D1074726

CATHOLIC INSTRUCTION IN IRELAND

MICHAEL TYNAN

Catholic Instruction in Ireland
1720-1950

THE O'REILLY/DONLEVY CATECHETICAL TRADITION

FOUR COURTS PRESS

The typesetting for this book was produced
by Computer Graphics Ltd, Dublin for
Four Courts Press, Kill Lane,
Blackrock, County Dublin.

ISBN 0-906127-82-3

Printed by A. Wheaton & Co. Ltd., Exeter

Contents

Foreword

My aim, in respect of the Irish language catechisms, has been to give the text as I found it. I have not tried to identify mistakes, only to indicate in fairness to the gallant printers of the time why they were made.

I refer throughout to the British Museum, as the institution was known when I first went in search of the catechisms. It is now, of course, the British Library.

I am one, I am sure, with all researchers in thanking the libraries that serve us with such skill and courtesy, the ones I refer to within the text and these others I have not mentioned, the libraries of Trinity College, Dublin, the Catholic University of Washington, D.C., the County Libraries of Cavan, Donegal, Monaghan, Wexford, and the Limerick City Reference Library.

I am obliged to Mr Patrick B. Lysaght of Limerick who has supplied me with book lore over many years, and to the computer department of the Limerick Diocesan Office, especially to Miss Mary Spain and Father Liam O'Sullivan.

M.T.

Introduction

Three factors contributed to the rapid spread of the Reformation: favourable political and social conditions, the personalities of the leaders and the invention of printing. Martin Luther, a publicist of genius, was quick to grasp the potential of the printing press for reaching the masses. He selected his media accordingly, the pamphlet and the cartoon for propaganda and, for instruction, the Bible, the hymn, and above all the catechism. Luther was not the inventor of the catechism — it was an inheritance from a united Christendom — but he developed and enhanced it as an educational medium and gave it a lease of life that Western man was to value for some 400 years. His *Small Catechism*, for children and simple folk, was enormously successful, running to tens of thousands of copies in 44 editions during his life time. He had by his death, in 1546, created something entirely new, a popular religious vernacular literature.

The Catholic Counter-Reformation was not ill-endowed either. It had princely and royal, indeed imperial backing; the printing presses were open to it; and early on, by force of its momentum, it had created Ignatius of Loyola and the Society of Jesus.

The Jesuits were denied the reformers' panache. They had no new worlds to offer, only old ones to defend; but they quickly showed themselves to be propagandists of no mean calibre and they avidly accepted 'the catechism' as the basic instrument of instruction. Some years before the Council of Trent had completed its work, and before the Council's own catechism had appeared,[1] the Jesuits had a blueprint for what a CounterReformation catechism ought to be. There is nothing so evocative of Tridentine things as an outline of rules for thinking with the Church appended to the *Spiritual Exercises* of St Ignatius.

Rules such as these:

To lay aside all private judgement.

To praise confession to a priest.

1 The reforming Council of Trent — the *Concilium Tridentinum* assembled in 1545. Prorogued twice, its work was not completed until 1564. The catechism commissioned by the Council, the *Roman Catechism*, appeared two years later.

To praise frequent hearing of Mass, also chants, psalms, and prolonged prayers both in and out of church.

To greatly praise Religious Orders, virginity and continence, and matrimony not so much as any of these.

To praise the relics of the saints, paying veneration to the relics and praying to the saints; and to praise likewise stations, pilgrimages, indulgences, jubilees, crusades and candles lighted in churches.

To praise enactments of the Church with regard to fasts and abstinences.

To arrive at truth in all things by being ready to believe that what seems to us white is black if the hierarchical Church so defines it.

It was this sort of thinking that made the Catholic as opposed to the Protestant neighbour whose doctrinal and ethical ambience was so directly contrary.

Indeed it was the rules as such, in their nitty-gritty detail, that, for and against, proved to be the stuff of religious life and controversy in the era. Every Christian — raised as he was on his catechism — was concerned in his formative years and in a measure throughout his life with issues such as the validity of the monastic concept, the nature of the Mass, the practice of confession, the veneration of saints, images and relics, the role of fast and abstinence in the life of the spirit, the question of indulgences, church ceremonial, the devotional practice of lighting candles or blessing oneself with holy water.

And not only did the Jesuits chart the course of the Counter-Reformation catechism: they became skilled catechism-makers themselves. Their two most famous catechists, Peter Canisius before Trent, and Robert Bellarmine after, produced what may well be described as the prototypal texts, the measure of what catechism came to mean for Tridentine Catholics, especially in northern Europe. They had the patronage of authority, their works instant best-sellers, rivalling Luther's and with comparable sales records. Our early catechism-makers, in exile on the continent, — the 'laborious and learned *Franciscans* of Louvain', as Donlevy was to call them, — leant heavily on the catechisms of Canisius and Bellarmine; and not for inspiration only: they copied from them freely. All the Irish language catechisms of the 17th century are rooted, directly or indirectly, in the Jesuit texts.

10

The *Teagasg Críosdaidhe* of Bonaventure O'Hussey, dating from 1608, adopts the structure of the Canisian catechisms and takes the substance of his exposition, in verse and prose, from Bellarmine's larger catechism, the *Copiosa Explicatio Doctrinae Christianae*. All the texts that follow are indebted to O'Hussey: Theobald Stapleton's *Catechismus*, bilingual in Latin and Gaelic, 1639; six years later, 1645, the *Parrthas an Anma* of Antony Gearnon, who casts the material in the question and answer form; John Dowley, in 1663, reverting to O'Hussey's style of prose and verse, in his *Suim Bhunadhasach an Teagaisg Chríosdaidhe* acknowledges his debt to the work of the Franciscan Fathers, naming Giollabríghde Ua heoghasa and the 'ughdar parrthuis an anma'. O'Hussey, especially, is Dowley's mentor: 'Do rin e mé díth'cioll san tshlíghe is fán modh labartha do fúair mé romham ag an athair Giollabríghde dogr/ múgadh go hairighthe ina dán . . .' Francis O'Molloy's *Lucerna Fidelium* of 1676 is indebted to O'Hussey too, and Donlevy's catechism, the last of the Irish catechisms from the continent, relates to O'Hussey through Antony Gearnon's *Parrthas* and prints O'Hussey's own verse abridgment.[2]

By way of these catechisms, our people in exile and in considerable measure those at home became familiar with the

2 *An Teagasg Críosdaidhe*, Bonabhentura Ó hEodhasa, O.F.M. a chum, Fearghal Mac Raghnaill, O.F.M. a chuir in eagar, Baile Átha Cliath, Institiúid Ard-Léinn Bhaile Átha Cliath, 1976; Coimisiún Láimhschríbhinní na hÉireann, Reflex Facsimiles IV, *The Catechismus of Theobald Stapleton*, Reproduced at the Ordnance Survey, Dublin, Stationery Office, 1945; *Parrthas an Anma*, Antoin Gearnon, O.F.M. a chum, Anselm Ó Fachtna, O.F.M. a chuir in eagar, Baile Átha Cliath, Institiúid Ard-Léinn Bhaile Átha Cliath, 1953; *Lucerna Fidelium*, Proinsias Ó Maolmhuaidh, O.F.M. a chum, Pádraig Ó Súilleabháin, O.F.M. a chuir in eagar, Dublin, Dublin Institute for Advanced Studies, 1962.

I am not aware of any modern editing of the Dowley catechism. There were two editions, both printed at Louvain from Gaelic founts, the second in 1728. This was printed along with 'The Elements of the Irish Language, Gramatically Explained', in 14 chapters, by H. Mac Curtin, who apologises for the abundance of abbreviations that continued in Irish books into the age of printing. These make the Dowley text difficult to read and more difficult to reproduce. I am obliged to an tAth. Mícheál Mac Craith, of the Irish Department in University College Galway, for the suggestion that the symbol used in the word or words 'dogr/múgadh' probably indicates the letters 'ea', so as to read 'do grean-múgadh' which means, according to Dinneen's dictionary 'to grapple with'. The preponderance of numerals, notable in all the catechisms, and the medieval preoccupation with their symbolism are perhaps specially evident in Dowley's. All uneven numbers, the number seven in particular, were given a peculiar religious significance. Dowley presents the section on the sacraments with a bold, dramatic heading: 'SEACHT — Sacramainte nuadaidh reachta Chriost'.

catechetical tradition of Canisius and Bellarmine. Nor were these Jesuits the only ones with an Irish connection in early days. Their confrère, Jeronimo de Ripalda, who with another Jesuit, Gaspar Astete, created the Spanish catechetical tradition that was to last till the end of the era, had touched Ireland even before them.

Ripalda's Catecismo de la *Doctrina Cristiana*, first published in Madrid in 1591, was translated into Irish by the Louvain Franciscan, Flaithrí Ó Maolchonaire in 1593, the Florence Conry who was to become the Archbishop of Tuam. It reached Ireland in manuscript in 1598, perhaps the first catechism in Irish to reach our shores: a faithful rendering of Ripalda's, with some neat adjustments skilfully done, a darling little text.[3]

The Jesuit catechisms sprung from the impetus which reform and counter-reform were giving to schooling; they were geared to the class-room and to the home, and since instruction has to be piecemeal, if not progressive, they varied in size. Canisius had three texts, two small, the *minimus* and the *minor*, and one elaborate exposition for the upper grades and adults. This latter text, the *maior* catechism, was the *Summa Doctrinae Christianae*, the first of the trilogy, and written at the command of Ferdinand I as an orthodox statement of the faith for his subjects. The Latin original was quickly translated into German. Bellarmine's work was organised in a different way, albeit amounting to the same thing. He had two catechisms, the Large for the teacher, the *Copiosa Explicatio*, and the Small for the child, the one more usually meant when there is talk of Bellarmine's catechism. Bellarmine's vernacular was Italian.[4]

All the catechisms in Irish we have mentioned as rooted in the Jesuit tradition were Large texts, with the exception of O'Hussey's

3   Brian Ó Cuív, 'Flaithrí Ó Maolchonaire's Catechism of Christian Doctrine' in *Celtica*, Vol. 1, Part 2, 1950.

4   St Peter Canisius (1542-1597). The *Summa* was published in 1555. In 1556 came the *Shortest Catechism*, an abridgment in Latin of the *Summa* adapted to the capacity of small boys; it came as an appendix to a boys' Latin Grammar. It had 59 questions. *The Smaller Catechism for Catholics*, with 124 questions followed in 1558. The German editions of this text were often richly illustrated with woodcuts and had pious exercises and meditations mingling with the barebone doctrinal instruction. This feature of Canisius's work appealed enormously to our catechism-makers in Louvain.

St Robert Bellarmine (1542-1621). Bellarmine's catechisms were prepared at the request of Pope Clement VIII and enjoyed papal backing throughout their history. The *Dottrina Cristiana Breve*, the child's book, in which the teacher asked the questions and the pupil replied, appeared in 1597. In 1598 the teacher's manual was published, the *Dichiarazione piú Copiosa della Dottrina Cristiana*, in which the pupil asks the questions and the teacher gives the answers.

12

little verse catechism and Florence Conry's *Ripalda*. The catechism promised by Trent, when it appeared two years after the Council had ended, was a Large text also, but somewhat different in aim from the catechisms we have been discussing: it was a source book · of instruction addressed to parish priests and geared to the pulpit.

The Roman Catechism, as it is so often called, was prescribed for our clergy as early as 1614 by the provincial synod of Armagh. A corresponding Tuam synod in 1660 directed every parish priest to have a copy. The work was available in English in 1687, the year before the fall of James II, published in London, *The Catechism for the Curats compos'd by the decree of the Council of Trent*. Another version appeared in London in 1852 and there were two translations published in Dublin in the earlier years of that century, one by E. and B. Dowling in 1816, the other by the Rev. Jeremy Donovan of Maynooth in 1829. Donovan's version became a standard work and had a considerable printing history for over a hundred years. Monsignor John Hagan's *Compendium of Catechetical Instruction*, Dublin, 1910, includes a translation of the Trent catechism by Hagan himself. The latest in English is the McHugh/Callan version, first published in America in 1923. These latter translations were inspired by revived interest in Sunday catechetical instruction prompted by the initiative of Pope St Pius X and proved very successful. A study of the influence of the Roman Catechism in our catechetical history, however, would likely establish that it was not considerable.

By the mid-18th century, after the fall of the Stuarts, we had acquired sufficient freedom to start on the foundations of a Tridentine establishment. The upbuilders of the emerging Irish Church had one enormous advantage. As a result of the popery laws the Catholic Church, by 1760, Maureen Wall notes, 'had more freedom to work out its destiny in Ireland than it had in many countries of Europe where Catholicism was the State religion, and where Catholic rulers constantly intervened in Church appointments and in Church policy'.[5] The result was the emergence of a Catholicism *du type Irlandais* that was a faithful reflection of the Counter-Reformation principle worked out by the Jesuits and canonized by the Council of Trent. The Ignatian blueprint for religious formation was to have an extraordinary influence on our society. Our people were impregnated by Ignatian thinking; they came to be steeped in its spirit and proved so consistent in reproducing it that, when the era was drawing to

5 *The Penal Laws; 1691-1760*, published for the Dublin Historical Association by Dundalgan Press, Dundalk, 1967, p. 67.

13

a close, they stood alone as a kind of affront to contemporary living in the West, even within the Church.

The catechism was not, indeed, the only influence in the creation of this phenomenon, but it was a major factor. With printing presses at our disposal, we took to catechisms in a big way, turning them out all sizes. The considerable Catholic printing industry developing throughout the second half of the 18th century was largely fed by catechism copy. But alas for poor Donlevy's ambition; he did not benefit from it. The large catechisms were almost exclusively in English and they came from across the Irish Sea, from English and Scottish authors of exceptional talent. The names that keep cropping up on the printing lists of the time, catechism-makers all, are John Gother, a 17th century writer, much admired by Dryden; the great Richard Challoner; Henry Turberville, a doughty Englishman from Staffordshire; John Joseph Hornyold, like Challoner, one of the early English Vicars Apostolic; the Benedictine, John Anselm Mannock; and the Scot, George Hay. The books of these catechists had a long printing history in Ireland. Some of them were warm favourites and had a profound influence.

Turberville's *Abridgment of the Christian Doctrine*, popularly known as the *Doway* from its origin in Douai College in the heroic days of the mid-17th century, was despite its title an elaborate text. A short version, in English and Irish, pp. 99, 12mo, was printed in Dublin in 1738. The full text was in ready circulation from early days until the second half of the last century. 'It was the high-water mark of catechetical instruction for children of the fifth class', Ronan states in his life of Fr Henry Young, *An Apostle of Catholic Dublin*; and he quotes a minute from the S.S. Michael and John's Register of 26 October 1828: 'That the lads who receive catechistical instruction in this Confraternity be not considered qualified to become teachers until they are fully instructed in the Large Abridgment and be otherwise particularly distinguished for their pious conduct'.[6]

The Poor Man's Catechism by Mannock, a fellow-countryman of Turberville's, was based on the *Doway* but essentially spiritual in orientation, a catechism of piety. The *Poor Man's* was to become a classic of prayerful instruction in the era. Its Dublin history began with a Cross and Wogan printing in 1794 and it had a steady run; I have seen a copy of a Duffy printing, 1858. Hay's works, the

6 Fr Myles V. Ronan's book, Dublin, Browne and Nolan, 1944, is a great help to students of our Tridentine formation and instruction. Rich with references to catechetical sources.

Sincere, Pious and *Devout Christian*, 'instructed in the Faith of Christ from the Written Word' laid the foundation of a fortune for the Dublin printer, Pat Wogan in the 1780's, and a hundred years later they were still going strong, supporting the publishing house of James Duffy and Co. Ltd., 15 Wellington Quay.[7] The catechetical form is used throughout these extensive studies, the exposition in great detail, all three dimensions of the faith brought into focus, doctrinal, scriptural, spiritual, and with engaging simplicity and elegance.

Yet, it was not the larger catechisms, with their limited reading public, but the small abridgments that really made the soul of our Tridentine people.

These were the little texts, all of them home-made, the booklets which meant 'my catechism' to so many generations. Some of them survived a span of more than 200 years, coming down to us unchanged or by way of a tradition they generated. The principle I have adopted for identifying a tradition is the survival in use in Ireland from the 18th century to the mid-20th of a catechism or group of related texts.

We had three such traditions:

1) The O'Reilly/Donlevy tradition
2) The tradition of the diocese of Ferns
3) The Butler catechisms.

The 1950's are chosen as the terminus because all the catechisms then in use in our school systems were gradually replaced by *A Catechism of Catholic Doctrine*, approved by the Archbishops and Bishops of Ireland and issued in the hope of its becoming a national text, which in one way or other it did. This catechism as published by M. H. Gill and Son Ltd of Dublin in the autumn of 1951 was to be our last contribution to the method of instruction that marked the Tridentine era.

On the eve of the publication of the national text catechisms from one or other of our three traditions were prescribed for use in every diocese.[8] The distribution was as follows:

7 For his story and that of his fellows see Thomas Wall's *The Sign of Doctor Hay's Head*, Dublin, Gill, 1958.

8 There were accommodations. In the diocese of Meath Dr William Moran's catechism was optional. Catechism in Irish was an issue. Two translations of the 'Maynooth' were available — Gill, and Dollard of Dublin, the latter by Dr Michael O'Flaherty, approved for the diocese of Elphin. But despite the Butler conquest of the West, the Tuam Catechism continued in use in the Connaught Gaeltacht. An t-Athair Peadar Ua Laoghaire's Irish catechism, a Butler text as it happens, was used in schools where everything was taught through Irish and in many others as part of the syllabus.

15

Catechisms of the Butler family were used in every diocese except four, the original text, as published by Archbishop James Butler of Cashel in 1777, surviving in Ossory, and in Meath where it was mistakenly ascribed to Bishop Plunket. Butler's Catechism had been 'revised, enlarged, approved and recommended by the Four R.C. Archbishops of Ireland as a General Catechism for the Kingdom' in 1802, eleven years after the author's death. This version, known as the *General Catechism* or, in the earlier lists, as the *Catechism of the Four Archbishops* was used in Down & Connor, Cashel & Emly, Cloyne, Ross and Kerry.

In 1882, the General was itself revised and issued as *The Maynooth Catechism* without Butler's name. This version was used in Armagh, Ardagh & Clonmacnoise, Kilmore, Dublin, Kildare & Leighlin, Killaloe, and in all the dioceses of the Province of Tuam — Tuam, Achonry, Clonfert, Galway, Killala, and Elphin.

Four other dioceses were using versions of *Butler*, with acknowledgement of title. Dromore had a *Shorter Catechism for the Use of Beginners* based on Butler's. Cork's *Butler* was 'Revised and Simplified', and Limerick shared with Waterford & Lismore a version described as 'Revised'.

More often, where the *General* and the *Maynooth* versions prevailed, two booklets were used, the full text and a shorter version, corresponding to the Smaller and Shortest texts of the Canisian tradition. The Cork and Limerick *Butlers* were similarly edited.

The original Ferns catechism is the work of William Devereux (1696-1771) who became parish priest of Drinagh, Co. Wexford in 1730 and Chancellor of Ferns in 1739. His name is associated also with the notable Kilmore Carols.[9] The original text of the catechism has not survived and the versions that have are somewhat laced with Butler interpolations. The tradition was carried from 1903 to our day by the catechism of Canon John Lennon, an extensive revision of Devereux's work. *Lennon* was remarkable for its length. Even the shorter edition, the abridgment, is formidable.

The other three dioceses of the four that had not been using Butler catechisms in the 1950's, Clogher, Derry and Raphoe adhered to the O'Reilly/Donlevy tradition, the subject of the present study.

---

9 Fr Joseph Ransom discusses the catechism in an article on 'The Kilmore Carols', in the Wexford historical journal, *The Past*, no 5, 1949. For the involvement of Devereux with the Kilmore carols, see Introduction to *The Wexford Carols* by Diarmaid O Muirithe and Seoirse Bodley, The Dolmen Press, 1982.

16

Bad cess to me, but it 'ud be a mortual sin, so it would, to let the poor boy die at all, an' him so far from home. For as the Catechiz says, 'There is but one faith, one Church, and one Baptism'. Well, the readin' that's in that Catechiz is mighty omprovin', glory be to God.

Jemmy M'Evoy's protector in Carleton's story, *The Poor Scholar*

1

Origins

The older of our two major traditions is Canisian in structure, if only by accident. There are three texts concerned: O'Reilly's, Donlevy's and the text we may call the Tuam Catechism, an abridgment of Donlevy's first published in 1839 'according to the resolution of the Archbishop of Tuam and the Bishops of that Province'. Here we have three catechisms planned on Canisian lines, in ascending grades of difficulty. You might begin with O'Reilly's as your *minimus* or 'Shortest Catechism', proceed to the Tuam text for your *minor* or 'Smaller Catechism' and round off with Donlevy's as *maior*, the tradition's *Summa*.

Each of these texts was published in Irish and in English, Donlevy's and the Tuam Catechism bilingually, page by page, the Irish on the left and the English on the right. Between them they could have made a reasonably satisfactory catechetical schema to the end of what we now call the second level. The trilogy was not of course conceived in this way, nor was it ever so used. The Tuam Catechism, the short Donlevy, was compiled to replace the parent text rather than to lead up to it. O'Reilly's is an entirely independent undertaking. One might indeed conclude from the texts themselves that O'Reilly compiled his catechism from Donlevy's as a short version of the larger text, but this is not so; there is sufficient evidence to convince that O'Reilly's work predates Donlevy's. The two catechisms nonetheless belong to the one tradition. Father Patrick Wallace discovered from a comparison of an O'Reilly text, P. Wogan's, 1802, and Renehan's 1848 edition of Donlevy's that 175 questions and answers in the O'Reilly manual, from a total of 189, are repeated substantially in Donlevy's.[1]

The history of Donlevy's catechism presents no problem. We have the first edition printed in Paris in 1742 by James Guerin and we can trace the subsequent history of the text step by step.

1 Ms. *Irish Catechesis: The Heritage from James Butler II Archbishop of Cashel 1774-1791.* A Dissertation submitted to the Faculty of The School of Religious Studies of the Catholic University of America for the degree of Doctor of Philosophy, 1975, p. 93.

The beginnings of the O'Reilly tradition, on the other hand, are less clear cut. The oldest copy of an O'Reilly catechism known to me is a photostat of the Irish text printed in Cork by Doncha O'Donnoghue in 1774. I have failed to trace an English text printed before the early 19th century. We are depending therefore on sources other than the texts themselves for information about the catechism's origin.

The evidence of the historian Renehan is contradictory. In his *Collections on Irish Church History* he states that at the beginning of his term as Bishop of Derry, which would be about 1739, O'Reilly 'published two excellent catechisms, one in English for use of the newly converted colonists, the other in Irish, the language at that time generally spoken in his diocese'.[2]

But in the preface to the edition of Donlevy's catechism which Renehan had published in 1848 he states that O'Reilly produced his Irish catechism 'about the time of his translation from the see of Derry to the Primacy of Armagh, in 1749'.

Pádraig Ó Súilleabháin OFM in an *Éigse* (XI, Part II) article, 'Roinnt Caiticeasmaí Gaeilge', cites C. Anderson as supporting this date in his *Historical sketches of the ancient native Irish and their descendants*, 1828.

From a chance reference, however, to which his attention was drawn by a colleague, Ó Súilleabháin discovered substantial evidence that O'Reilly's Irish catechism appeared considerably earlier than 1749 or even 1739.

A Protestant Rector, one J. Richardson, published in Dublin in 1727 a tract he called *The great folly, superstition, and idolatry of pilgrimages in Ireland*. On pages 116-7 of this provocative tract there is a left-handed compliment paid to the parish priest of Cavan who, at the time, happened to be our O'Reilly:

And one Thing very remarkable hath occured of late, much to the Commendation of the Popish Priest of *Cavan*: In a Catechism, which (as I am told) he composed and distributed, not long since, among his People and others: He gives up the worshipping of Saints, in these Words, which , to do him Justice, I shall insert here, as they are therein expressed by himself, by way of Question and Answer.

C. Ionn coír Muire Mhathair no na naoimh dadharadh?

F. Ní coir, do bhrígh gurab onoir so dlithear do Dhia amhain.

C. Ion ccoisgion an Aithnesi, Onoir do thabhart do na Naoimh?

2 *Collections on Irish Church History.* From the MSS of the late V. Rev. Laurence F. Renehan, D.D., President of Maynooth College. Edited by the Rev. Daniel McCarthy. Vol. 1. Irish Archbishops. Dublin: C. M. Warren, 21 Upper Ormond Quay; Thomas Richardson and Son, 9 Capel Street, 1861, p. 101.

19

F. Ni choisgionn, do bhrigh nach anann an Onoir do bheirmid doibh, agas do dhia: Oir onoramaoid iad amhain mur Chairde, agus mur sheirbhiseacha De.

The passage quoted occurs in the second lesson of Part II of O'Reilly's catechism. It is substantially, almost word for word, the same in all our printings, both English and Irish. Ó Súilleabháin compares with an 1802 version of the catechism and finds that they tally exactly, except that 'Oir' is missing from the second answer and that 'dessle' follows 'herveesacha' in that sentence. 'Deesle' i.e., 'dilse', Ó Súilleabháin observes, is a 'focal a mbeadh súil agat leis'. It occurs consistently in the English texts where the passage runs as follows:

Q. Is it lawful to adore the blessed Virgin or the saints?

A. No: for by adoration is here meant the honour due to God alone.

Q. Does this commandment forbid us to honour the saints?

A. No: for the honour we give them is different from that which we pay to God. We honour the saints as friends and faithful servants of God.

I feel that nobody aware of the fidelity with which our catechisms have been handed down would hesitate to accept that Richardson took the passage from O'Reilly's catechism as we know it and that, accordingly, the text existed at the time this good man was so worried about Catholic superstition and idolatry.

It seems not unreasonable to conclude also that Donlevy had O'Reilly's catechism before him. True, he does not acknowledge this in his preface, although he refers to 'little *Abridgments, meerly* calculated for *Beginners*' and 'those little short *Catechisms* by heart'. His method, however, was to quote his doctrinal sources, the scriptures, the decrees and catechism of Trent and other Church decisions rather than the catechetical texts from which we know he borrowed.

I am dependent on the researches of others for light on the careers of O'Reilly and Donlevy and, apart from the bond of their handing down the same catechetical tradition, I can discover only one link between them, and that tenuous enough, the Irish College in Paris. Donlevy, the older of the two by about ten years, was born in 1680 and died in 1746. For the twenty-four years before his death, he was the prefect or dean, as we would say in my seminarian tradition, of the young men who came to study in the Irish College. He states in the preface to the catechism that he had been thirty-one years from the homeland as he was writing, all this time presumably in the Irish College. I have no knowledge of his career before that.

20

O'Reilly was born about 1690 and died in 1758 as Archbishop of Armagh. He was educated in Paris, returned without delay to his native diocese of Kilmore, laden with academic honours, and set for a notable career in the Irish Church or 'mission' as it was called at the time. He was Parish Priest of Cavan and Vicar General of Kilmore very early in his career. He was appointed Bishop of Derry in 1739 and became Primate ten years later.

2

Primate O'Reilly handing down ...

The O'Reilly catechism has come down to us more faithfully in both versions than have the spelling and structure of the author's name. Renehan and the historian of Breiffne, Philip O'Connell, consistently use the form 'O'Reilly'. But all the printings in English I have seen, the Derry edition only excepted, attribute the catechism to 'the Most Rev. Dr. Reilly'. The Gaelic printings generally omit the author's name from the title page, except in Munster where several printings attribute the catechism to Archbishop Butler.

The future Primate was evidently baptised 'Reily'. In a letter of approbation prefixed to Primate Hugh MacMahon's *Jus Primatiale Armacanum*, he so signs himself, 'Michael Reily, Juris utriusq. Doctor, et Vs. Gs. Ks.' The abbreviations are carefully interpreted by O'Connell to mean 'Juris utriusque Doctor, et Vicarius Generalis Kilmorensis'.[1] He was born in the County Cavan and in the diocese of Kilmore. I have discovered nothing about his early years and there is some conflict of evidence about his ecclesiastical education. I learn from Hugh Fenning's *The Undoing of the Friars of Ireland* that O'Reilly was trained for the priesthood in the Irish College, Paris.[2] Both Renehan and O'Connell (the latter no doubt relying on the former) claim the Propaganda College in Rome as the place of his ecclesiastical formation. Renehan states that Dr O'Reilly studied in Rome, 'in the Propaganda I think'; but the evidence is vague, and if he did he may have studied there as a priest, following his ordination in Paris.[3] However, the Paris connection is well established and it is a link with Donlevy.

The diocese of Kilmore had been without a bishop for many years and was being administered by the Bishop of Clogher, Dr Hugh MacMahon, when O'Reilly came home. No doubt it was the young man's brilliance and rich promise that secured him the

1 Philip O'Connell, *Diocese of Kilmore*, Dublin, 1957, pp. 459f. My source for the narrative which follows is O'Connell's book, except where otherwise stated.
2 Hugh Fenning OP, 'A Study of the Novitiate Question in the Eighteenth Century', Louvain, 1972. For the evidence of O'Reilly's Paris connection, p. 156, 166f.
3 Renehan, op. cit., p. 100.

parish of Cavan and the vicar-generalship of the diocese, which he virtually ruled until 1730. This was the period during which the catechism was 'distributed'.

In 1728 the bishopric of Kilmore was restored when a young Dominican, Michael MacDonogh, was appointed by Benedict XIII, who happened to be a Dominican himself. This was a blow to O'Reilly. One gathers from Renehan and O'Connell that he would have been the choice of Hugh MacMahon, who had continued to administer Kilmore when he left Clogher for Armagh. The Primate, however, was able to salve O'Reilly's wound, for he had in his gift the parish of Drogheda and the vicar-generalship of Armagh, both of which he promptly bestowed on the displaced administrator when the youthful Dr MacDonogh arrived in 1730 to take over his diocese.

O'Reilly held his posts in Armagh until 1739 when he was appointed Bishop of Derry by papal brief of April 24th in that year. Derry had been without a bishop since the early 17th century, and judging by a report on the Catholic structure issued in 1731 by the Protestant bishop of the diocese, O'Reilly's inheritance was inconsiderable:

There are in ye Diocese of Derry only nine Mass-houses, Mass being said in most places sub dio, or under some sort of shed, built up occasionally to shelter ye priest from ye weather.

Four of ye said Mass-houses were built since ye 1st of King George ye 1st (i.e., 1714); ye rest before, and all mean, inconsiderable buildings.

O'Reilly was to spend some ten years coping as best he might with this predicament. In 1749 he became Primate. His patron, Primate Hugh MacMahon, died in 1737 and was succeeded by his two nephews, Bernard MacMahon first, and his brother Ross following, both of whom had been bishops of Clogher. Bernard was Primate for ten years, to 1747, Ross for just a year. On the death of Primate Ross MacMahon, O'Reilly's turn came. His admirers in the college in Paris, Fenning notes, zealously promoted his candidature. They wrote to James III, who had the nomination of bishops in his gift, praising their candidate's virtues and achievements. 'They spoke of his reformation of Kilmore, which he found the worst and left as the best regulated diocese in the kingdom. In their opinion, and they asserted it from a positive sense of duty, O'Reilly could most justly be called the Charles Borromeo of Ireland'.[4] The brief of appointment from Benedict XIV is dated 23 January 1749.

The penal climate in which O'Reilly worked and taught his

4 Fenning, op. cit., p. 157f, 176.

catechisms is no doubt accurately described in this somewhat flamboyant passage from Renehan:

The blaze of persecution not regularly fed by the blood of the martyrs had been for some (time) gradually expiring, and had at length dwindled into a rambling flame, showing itself today in one county, tomorrow in another. The clergy, it is true, dared not avow their character, nor the Catholic slaves shew dissatisfaction with their chains, but while they remained concealed, no reptiles were systematically employed to dislodge them from their retreats, unless, perhaps, now and again to gratify the caprice or malice, or bigotry of some little local persecutor.

There was in fact a resurgence of active persecution for a brief period in the mid-1740s during the viceroyship of the Duke of Devonshire. O'Reilly had to leave his diocese at the time and hide in Dublin, directing his affairs in Derry, so Renehan says, 'from an alley in the metropolis'. During his Armagh days he lived in a small cottage in Termonfeckin, near Drogheda, and is said even then to have had to lie concealed from time to time in a narrow loft under the thatch.[5] Winds of change were, however, beginning to blow. An incident during his primacy has been well researched. In April 1756 he was arrested along with a number of his clergy who had assembled for the blessing and distribution of the Holy Oils. The arrest, on a patently trumped-up charge, was reluctantly carried out by James Hamilton, Viscount Limerick, who had the Archbishop and the clergy taken to his house where he examined them politely and let them go. Hamilton was convinced that legal changes were overdue, and it was his experience as a magistrate in this instance that led him to make proposals for a new system of registering priests.[6] A bill he brought before Parliament was twice defeated, but the strength of popery was too obviously becoming a political reality calling for some ascendancy accommodation.

Trouble with the law was not the only source of the Primate's frustrations. He had his share of internal problems too arising from a disorganised ecclesiastical structure. He had hardly landed in Armagh when he discovered that one John Brullaughan, who had figured disreputably in an incident involving Bishop MacDonogh of Kilmore, with no great credit to the bishop either, had been appointed Bishop of Derry. The Archbishop succeeded just in time in having the appointment quashed.[7]

5 Ambrose Coleman, *Cath. Encycl.*, Vol. 1, New York, 1909, p. 732.
6 See John Brady, 'Proposals to Register Irish Priests 1756-7' in *Irish Ecclesiastical Record*, April 1962. Ref. to *Arch. Hib.*, XVI 90, Appendix.
7 Hugh Fenning OP, 'Laurence Richardson OP, Bishop of Kilmore, 1747-1753' in *I.E.R.*, March 1968.

O'Reilly had to be a man of character to support his reforming zeal, building up the shattered dioceses of Kilmore, Derry and Armagh, and engaged throughout his episcopate and especially as Primate in the work of reforming the 'mission' at large. He was at the heart of the struggle between the secular and regular clergy that led to 'the undoing of the Friars of Ireland', abolishing their Irish novitiates. He was, too, a subtle and forceful ecclesiastical politician, the other role in which Hugh Fenning has assessed his merits and his faults.[8]

But what sort of a person was he? Fenning regrets that we know so little about him. 'There seems to have been in his life an unusually close connection between his experiences and his ideas, which is something that only a proper biographical study can bring out'. Lacking this, however, we can only make do with what is available. Fenning's own judgment is that of those who pursued the regular clergy so relentlessly Michael O'Reilly was at once 'the most powerful and honest'.[9]

He was also an impatient and insensitive man, and there is evidence of imprudent handling of the clergy thwarting his reforming zeal. 'He was a most rigid disciplinarian', Bishop Edmund Derry of Dromore said of the Archbishop, 'and it was his practice to surprize the priests on Sundays, whom, if he discovered the children committed to their care were not instructed in the catechism, he publicly rebuked with unfeeling severity'.[10]

He was, of course, particularly concerned about catechism and not only because he had written a catechism himself but because of the urgent need for Catholic instruction and the limited opportunities for providing it. It was the age of the ascendant Protestant Charter Schools system and there was a feeling abroad among the reformers within the Catholic camp, like O'Reilly, that much more might be done about the provision of Catholic schooling.[11] Nonetheless, 'unfeeling severity' ill becomes an Archbishop. One wonders, indeed, why this rigidity of discipline should have been so widespread in the ecclesiastical administration

8 In 'The Irish Dominican Province at the Beginning of its Decline (1745-1761)', from *Archivum Fratrum Praedicatorum*, Vol. XLV, Rome, 1975.

9 *The Undoing of the Friars of Ireland*, op. cit., Introduction, p. 9, pp. 52, 156, and *passim*.

10 See note by J.D. in *I.E.R.*, Third Series, Vol.XIII, p. 569 and Renehan, op. cit.

11 See Fenning, op. cit., *passim*. On the Charter School system, see Corcoran, *State Policy in Irish Education*, Dublin, 1916, *Selected Texts on Education Systems in Ireland*, 1918 pp. 56-66; and *A protestant catechism, showing the principal errors of the church of Rome*, Dublin, 1740, widely used in the Charter Schools.

of O'Reilly's time.[12] Did it spring from the harsh realities of the age, or from the authoritarian society in which people were cast in 'superior' and 'inferior' moulds, or did it reveal a Jansenist temper of mind?

At any rate the severity provoked so bitter a reaction that we find Renehan commenting on reports that 'the violent demeanour' of some of the clergy brought the poor Archbishop prematurely to his grave. But if we can believe a touching tradition recorded by Cardinal Moran[13] about him in the role of catechist, he seems to have mellowed before his death, at least towards the children. Moran tells of a visit he paid to the diocese of Armagh and of his being conducted to the place where the Primate lived, where

In the adjoining orchard a fine old apple tree is pointed out, under which, like St. Philip Neri on the Janiculum, the Primate was wont to gather the little children around him to instruct them in the catechism.

Perhaps isolation and loneliness had bred some tenderness. He died in 1758 and was buried in the Chord cemetery outside St Laurence's Gate at Drogheda. O'Connell regrets 'that no inscription marks the resting-place of this illustrious and venerable Kilmore ecclesiastic'. But O'Reilly had built his own monument. The catechism was to keep his memory alive for just about two hundred years.

O'Connell records the testimony of Dr Derry, the Bishop of Dromore we have quoted already, to the progress of the O'Reilly catechisms, stating that the Archbishop

published two Catechisms, one in Irish, the other in English; and though there have been many others written and printed since that period, his work (particularly in Ulster) has the ascendant.

Derry, who became Bishop of Dromore in 1801, died in 1819. Renehan, who lived in 1857, brings the record further:

So solid, accurate and well adapted to the wants of the people was the instruction conveyed in these little abridgments of the Christian doctrine, that they were immediately introduced into the other dioceses of the province, and although several other catechisms have been since

12 See A. Cogan in *Diocese of Meath*, Vol. III, Dublin, 1870. Dr Plunket, Bishop of Meath, 1779-1827, a zealous reformer in his generation, would jot down his comments at confirmation time and leave them with the parish priest who was to make a copy and return the original to the bishop. Throughout a large range of quotes there is not a single word of praise. Yet, as the record shows, he had inherited a viable diocesan structure of some sixty parishes and a catechetical system that was not ineffective.

13 *The Catholics under the Penal Laws in the Eighteenth Century*, London, 1899, p. 26, quoted by Patrick Wallace, op. cit. Ms., p. 91.

published, yet even to this day, O'Reilly's retains the greatest share of circulation at least in Ulster.

Other catechisms there were, some of them establishing considerable if limited traditions of their own,[14] and the Butler texts in their varied editions had captured most of the market by the beginning of the present century, but in parts of Ulster the O'Reilly tradition was destined to survive to the end of the era.

14   One of these in Ulster, by Dr James Pulleine, the Titular Dean of Dromore diocese, *An Teagasg Críosdaidhe Angoidhleig*, was very successful. A 1748 printing in the British Museum and in the National Library, a printing dated 1782. See the *I.E.R.*, June 1947 for a study of the latter by Francis McPolin, 'An Old Irish Catechism from Oriel'. The Kirwan catechism in Connaught belongs to the same category, having created a tradition in manuscript and print throughout the first half of the 19th century, but not surviving to our time. And in Limerick, unlike Kirwan's which is in Irish only, a bilingual text, Bishop Young's catechism, with a life span comparable to Kirwan's. The Kirwan and Young catechisms are related to the tradition we are studying. An edition of the Kirwan text claims that 'it is more explicit than any other Irish Catechism, next to Donlevy's, although containing matters that are not in that Catechism'. Young borrowed from O'Reilly; his first lesson is clearly based on O'Reilly's opening chapter and the structure of the catechism is in the O'Reilly/Donlevy tradition.

3

O'Reilly's Catechism

O'Reilly's catechism is truly an abridgment, the sort of thing envisaged by Donlevy 'for Children at their Horn-book', not child-centred by any manner of means and with none of the palliatives Canisius so lovingly provided, but it was a scrap of a thing compared to the abridgments that were to succeed it. The questions are short, even blunt, and they provoke on the whole a corresponding reply.

Q. Is it necessary to have faith?

A. It is; for without faith it is impossible to be saved.

Q. Is the Father God?

A. He is.

Q. Is there any of these three persons older or better than the other?

A. No; they are equal in everything.

Q. Is it lawful to tell a lie for a good end?

A. No; for no reason or motive can excuse a lie.

Q. What kind of gluttony is most sinful?

A. Drunkenness.

Some of the formulas are no more than medieval-style enumerations: the three theological virtues, the four sins crying to heaven for vengeance, the seven spiritual and seven corporal works of mercy, the eight beatitudes, the nine ways whereby one may be guilty of another's sin, the fifteen mysteries of the rosary .

When called on to expound, O'Reilly leaves no doubt about his meaning.

Q. What do these commandments forbid?

A. The one forbids us all carnal knowledge except between husband and wife. The other forbiddeth even the desire of such carnal knowledge.

Q. Are smutty discourses, wanton looks, and lewd kisses forbidden?

A. Yes, they are; as also any unchaste touching of one's self or others.

Q. Is it a breach of these commandments to have impure thoughts, when one has no desire to commit the action?

A. Yes, it is, if we entertain such thoughts wilfully and with pleasure.

He is not without style either. His concept of relations between husband and wife is sensitively judged and memorably put.

Q. How must a husband behave towards his wife?

A. He must use her lovingly, carefully and tenderly, like a part of his own body, as Christ doth his spouse, the Church.

Q. How must a wife behave towards her husband?

A. With love, respect, and submission, as the Church does towards Christ.

There is one jarring note, an echo perhaps of Jansenism, but reflecting a climate of ecclesiastical discipline not peculiarly Tridentine. Here the holy sacrament is presented in the shadow of damnation, the supreme gift of love administered by a punitive Church.

Q. Do those who go to communion in a state of mortal sin receive the body of Christ?

A. Yes; they receive it to their own damnation, as Judas did.

Q. Why is it a cause of damnation to them?

A. Because they receive it in a bad state, and thereby commit a most horrible sacrilege.

Q. How does the Church punish those who, having arrived at the years of discretion, confess not for a whole year, nor receive the Blessed Sacrament within that period, especially at Easter.

A. The great Council of Lateran orders, they shall be debarred of divine service and entrance into the church during life, and deprived of Christian burial at their death.

The catechism is planned on the early Jesuit lines, as we have been saying, with the four parts of the Tridentine Catechism — the four 'things', the keire nehe of the early Irish printings, which enable us to know, love and serve God, and so gain eternal life — followed by the sundry extras conveniently tagged and numbered. These four essential parts of the Christian Doctrine are identified in the first lesson:

> To believe firmly whatever God has revealed and declared to us by his Church.

29

To keep the commandments of God and of his Church.

To receive the sacraments with the requisite dispositions.

To put our whole trust in God, and to have recourse to him frequently.

The order is peculiar to O'Reilly and it got him into trouble when it came to aligning the parts with the theological virtues of faith, hope and charity, according to the tradition he was following. In both Jesuit texts, *Faith* (the Apostles' Creed) and *Hope* (the Lord's Prayer and the Hail Mary) are followed by *Charity*, embracing the commandments, as it does so evidently in Gospel teaching. The seven sacraments are next, and then the loose ends, sin and good works, virtues and vices, beatitudes, counsels and so on. O'Reilly had not indeed forgotten about charity as the vital force in obedience when he was teaching the commandments. In the first lesson of his Part II he declares the love of God and neighbour to be an abridgment of the commandments, makes an act of the love of God and considers 'wherein consists the love we owe our neighbour'. What he did forget was that, consistently with his plan, the virtue of charity should have been here defined, whereas it turns up as such for the first time in the fourth part, and among the extras, where the theological virtues are enumerated, then only equipped with its due definition, in a vacuum, with the catechism nearly complete and as if love had nothing to do with *caritas*.

There is an interesting connection between O'Reilly's text and the English 'penny' catechism tradition, closely modelled on Bellarmine's and surviving to this day in *A Catechism of Christian Doctrine*, Approved by the Archbishops and Bishops of England and Wales.[1] The O'Reilly tradition and the English 'penny', a catechism that was to show considerable development, began as far as we can trace them in the twenties of the 18th century. Marron, in his history of the English tradition points out that the progenitor of the English catechism known to us, the *Short Abridgment of Christian Doctrine*, is the first catechism in the English language to open with the question, 'Who made you?'[2] O'Reilly opens in the same way, as does Butler, by identifying God as our Creator. Compare O'Reilly's with the English catechism's latest printing to hand, (Catholic Truth Society, London, 1971):

1 A connection extending also to the catechetical tradition of the diocese of Ferns.

2 Marron, Dom J.S., O.S.B., in *The Sower*, October — December 1937.

English text —

Q. Who made you?

A. God made me.

Q. Why did God make you?

A. God made me to know Him, love Him and serve Him in this world, and to be happy with Him for ever in the next.

O'Reilly's text —

Q. Who created you, and made you in the world?

A. God.

Q. Why did God create you?

A. To know Him, love Him, and serve Him, and by that means to gain everlasting life.

In the early texts of the English tradition, moreover, the *Short Abridgment* catechisms[3] a lesson on sin appears between the lessons on the commandments and the sacraments, and this is what O'Reilly does: he has a couple of chapters on sin at the end his Part II. O'Reilly's lessons are more elaborate than the *Short Abridgment* version. The wording is different also, but the structure is about the same, a definition of sin, the distinction between original and actual, the seven capital or deadly sins, the four sins that cry to heaven for vengeance and the nine ways in which one can be responsible for another's sin. In the English text as it comes down to us the first lesson on sin is given with the teaching of the tenth article of the Creed, 'The forgiveness of sins', and as if to hold on to the connection this order was followed in the Derry revision of O'Reilly.

O'Reilly's catechism is something less than two hundred questions and answers, but his work includes two other doctrinal studies, *A Catechism of the Sacrament of Confirmation* and *An Abridgment of Faith*. The *Abridgment of Faith* 'to be said on Sundays, at the Parish Mass, and in private Families', may well be described as a Tridentine Creed.

The *Abridgment* is quite lengthy, some 900 words, and it is run off in all the printings, Irish and English, in two paragraphs, without taking breath, no doubt to save space. I should like to record it entirely, in roomier paragraphs to allow for easy breathing; for this is pure Tridentine air. It might be recited once a year,

3 *A Short Abridgment of Christian Doctrine: For the Instruction of Beginners.* Printed in the Year, 1745.

like the Creed of Athanasius used to be in the old Roman Breviary on Trinity Sunday, perhaps on the Feast of St Oliver Plunkett!

There is but one only God, who is a pure spirit, eternal and infinite, by whom heaven and earth were created and who is Sovereign Lord thereof.

There are three persons in God, the Father, the Son, and the Holy Ghost; the Father is God, the Son is God, and the Holy Ghost is God, yet there are not three Gods, but one only God, in three persons, equal in all things, which mystery is called the Holy Trinity.

The Son of God, who is the second person of the Blessed Trinity, became man (he alone, not the Father, nor the Holy Ghost) in the chaste womb of the Blessed Virgin Mary, to deliver us from sin and redeem us from damnation, to which we are liable by the sin of our first father Adam. This mystery was performed by the operation of the Holy Ghost, the five and twentieth day of March, a long time after the creation of the world; for the Son of God dying was always God, not always man; He became man without ceasing to be God, and will be eternally God and man together.

It is the Son of God, made man, whom we call Jesus Christ. He was born at midnight in a stable in extreme poverty. The feast of his divine birth is called Christmas. He lived three and thirty years wherein He has taught us the truths necessary for salvation, and furnished us with examples of all kinds of virtue, doing good to every one, living humbly, poorly, and painfully, bearing patiently for the sins of mankind all the miseries of this life, sin only excepted. At the end of His life He was nailed to a cross on which He expired to satisfy God's justice for our sins, and to purchase for us all the graces necessary for our salvation. The memory of His death and passion is solemnized on Good Friday, and every spiritual good we have in this life, or hope for in the next, is owing to his life, passion, and death; the third day after His death He arose gloriously from the dead; forty days after His resurrection He ascended into heaven, which day is called Ascension day. Ten days after which, being Pentecost, or Whit Sunday, He sent His Holy Spirit to His apostles and His Church.

At the end of the world He will come to judge all mankind, who must appear at the general resurrection before Him in the same bodies which they had upon this earth; to the just He will bestow heaven and the wicked He will send to hell.

He has instituted seven sacraments, whereby the merits of His passion and death are applied to us:— Baptism, Confirmation, Penance, Eucharist, Extreme Unction, Holy Orders, and Matrimony.

By Baptism we are made Christians and children of God; it is by it we are cleansed from original sin. By Confirmation we receive the Holy Ghost and are strengthened in faith.

By Penance we receive in faith, and in the purpose of leading a Christian life, forgiveness of those sins committed by us after Baptism. To receive this sacrament in a good state, one should examine his

32

conscience, conceive a great sorrow for having offended God, who is infinitely good; resolve firmly to avoid sin, and all occasions thereof; reconcile himself firmly and from his heart to his offending neighbour: repay the injury done him in his honour and substance, and satisfy God in performing the penance laid on him by the priest, and withal bearing patiently the evils of this life in the spirit of repentance.

In the holy sacrament of the Eucharist are contained the body and blood, the soul and divinity of Jesus Christ Our Lord, under the appearance of bread and wine; to receive worthily, one must be free from mortal sin, and resolve to shun the occasions thereof; he must have a great desire of leading a holy and truly Christian life.

Extreme Unction helps us to die well. Holy Orders gives power and grace to exercise holy offices. Marriage gives the grace to those engaged in it of mutual and holy love, and of educating their children according to the law of God.

There is but one true Church governed by the Holy Ghost, which every Christian is bound to obey; our holy Father the Pope is the visible Head thereof.

It is not enough for salvation to be a member of the holy Catholic Church; one must besides fulfil the commandments of God, which are reduced to these two principles — to love God with all his heart, and with all his soul, with all his strength, and his neighbour as himself.

In the introduction to his Confirmation catechism, O'Reilly bewails the fact that the faithful are deprived of those 'whose province it is to administer this sacrament', attributing the misfortune to sin and urging the people to desire the sacrament they are unable to receive.

I thought proper to publish this short Catechism concerning this sacrament, in order that the people should know what it is; and that considering its value, and their loss in being deprived of it, they might pray to the merciful God to supply the want of it by administering to them invisibly what they have an ardent desire of receiving if possible, and endeavour to keep themselves free from mortal sin, with whch the Holy Spirit will never dwell in a soul — Wisd. 1.4.

He ends by appealing to his 'fellow-labourers in Christ' to teach and explain the catechism to young and old, 'and that in the language of the hearers'.

The catechism is in four lessons, with some forty questions and answers, explaining the nature, effects and ceremonies of the sacrament and the dispositions required for receiving it well. Evidence again of a punishing zeal, in respect of parents who neglect to present their children: the Church, they are warned, formerly inflicted 'a penance of three whole years, which shows how great a sin it is to neglect Confirmation when it can be had'.

It seems excessive, too, to be warning against the 'horrible sacrilege' of knowingly receiving the sacrament more than once when the question at issue is whether one may have the chance of receiving it at all. But by and large the catechism is further testimony to O'Reilly's not inconsiderable catechetical skills and to the force and beauty with which he is able to invest his teaching:

Q. What doth the oil of olives signify?

A. It signifies the unction and abundance of grace which the person confirmed receives, and the sweetness he ought to be endued with.

Q. What does the balsam represent?

A. It puts us in mind of the obligation we are under of being the good odour or scent of Jesus Christ, by an exemplary life.

Q. Why is the Sign of the Cross made on the forehead?

A. 1st. To let the person confirmed know that he should not be ashamed to confess the faith of Jesus Christ, nor to lead a Christian life. 2ndly. To signify the strict obligation he is under of making outward profession of his faith, when the glory of God requires it, even at the expense of his life's wordly substance and honour.

Q. Why is the cross made with holy chrism?

A. To show that the crosses of Christians are sweetened by the comfort that God gives to those that suffer for his sake.

In the last instruction, confirming Confirmation itself, indignation provoked by affront to the faith charges O'Reilly's eloquence. One recalls the doughty Turberville for whom also Confirmation was so vividly a 'persecution' sacrament. O'Relly puts in a fighting finish, calling on those endowed with the graces of the sacrament for gentleness towards the afflicted, loyalty to the truth and readiness to endure.

Q. How may we know that the confirmed makes good use of the graces received in this sacrament?

A. If besides practising the things already mentioned, we find him inclined to compassionate the miserable and comfort the afflicted; if he abhors lies and insincerity, speaks according to his heart, opposes blasphemy and injurious discourses belched by libertines against the honour of Jesus Christ or His saints and servants; if, in fine, he is prepared to suffer all hardships and extremities sooner than renounce his faith — if he overcome the temptations and amusements of the world, the devil, and his own flesh, enemies no less dangerous than the racks and torture of persecutors.

So much for the formal instruction of O'Reilly's catechisms. There is another dimension to his work in which one may detect a genuinely Canisian note. He makes some effort to blend the devout life with his doctrinal formulations. He does it within the catechism text itself, as space allows, and with his extensive collection of prayers and practices of piety. Scholastic-wise he defines a virtue, and — 'make an Act of Faith' — forthwith demands its exercise in prayer. He tends to avoid the dichotomy between doctrine and practice which is evident in the Butler tradition.

Hearken unto the voice of my prayer, my King and my God, for I will pray to Thee; my voice shalt Thou, O Lord, hear in the morning — Psalm v.3,4.
   In the evening and at noon, will I address Him, and He will hear my voice — Psalm liv. 18.

The ideal Tridentine day begins and ends with private and family devotions. As initiated by O'Reilly and his kin, it counted up to a piety, formidable and a trifle stark, albeit warmed by the tender devotion to the persons of Jesus and Mary. Morning acts of adoration, thanksgiving, love, 'oblation' — what later came to be known as the 'Morning Offering' — of souls and bodies, hearts, minds and wills, thoughts, words and actions to God's greater honour and glory. A pause to consider the prospect of the day, then the 'Act of Good Resolution', the Pater and the Ave, the Apostles' Creed, the popular Litany of the Most Holy Name of Jesus, and so to work with this glowing invocation on your lips:

O Sovereign Lord, Jesus Christ, who saidst: 'Ask and it shall be given you; seek and you shall find; knock and it shall be opened to you', give us, Thy petitioners, an ardent inclination and desire of being inflamed with Thy most divine love; to the end that we may with our souls and hearts entirely love Thee, and with our tongues give continual praise and thanksgiving unto Thee, who livest and reignest with the Father and the Holy Ghost, one God, world without end. Amen.

Evening prayers follow a similar pattern. Acts of adoration and thanksgiving, examination of conscience, pause to conceive a great grief and horror for sin, the act of contrition, family prayers for intercession and protection, to God, the holy angels, the holy patron. The Litany of the Blessed Virgin Mary of Loreto is said. Prayers for the faithful departed and this invocation, the closing antiphon to the *Nunc dimittis* from the Compline of the Roman Breviary:

Preserve us, O Lord, waking, and protect us sleeping, that we may watch with Christ, and rest in peace.

Sleep itself was not without its awesome reminder, a sign of death for the pious mind — 'seeing', as the closing prayers warn us, we are uncertain going to bed this night whether we shall ever rise from thence ....

Later on in our tradition there was to come a rich flowering of 'devotions' based on parish sodalities, and on churches vastly different from the wretched Mass-houses of O'Reilly's day. But the inward-looking, soul-searching spirituality he is teaching here, all conscience and confession of sins, is the essential Tridentine thing. It was to gain an enormous hold on our people, this life-style in the shadow of the cloister, the faith conceived as Thèrése of Lisieux did the vocation of a Carmelite, as a life of thought.

4

The English texts

It is unfortunate that in the one personal contact we have with
O'Reilly himself, in the preamble to his Confirmation catechism,
he manages to tell us nothing really worth while about the origins
of the texts. It might appear on the face of it that he wrote the
Confirmation catechism when he was parish priest of Cavan and
vicar general of Kilmore, a see without a bishop. On the other
hand it may be argued that he could have written it after his
consecration. The times were uncertain, bishops could be impeded
in the discharge of their duties and there were bishops insufficiently
committed. Cogan's *Diocese of Meath* shows how few of the faithful
received the sacrament about the time Dr Plunket began his
ministry in 1778, a generation after O'Reilly's time. The
Confirmation catechism, moreover, seems to be associated with
the English O'Reilly; I have never found it in full in an Irish text,
nor have I found it at all in the Ulster Irish versions.

We do not know, of course, when the English version appeared.
There is no evidence whatever that it appeared at the same time
as the Irish version. Nor do we know for that matter whether the
Irish catechism was actually published in the sense of being printed
in the 1720's. Dean Richardson, who provides us with that precious
fragment, speaks of a catechism composed by the popish priest
of Cavan and *distributed* — the italic is mine — among his people.
He does not say it was printed, and more likely it was not but
issued in manuscript. One must take account also of the repeated
references we have been considering to the origin of the work when
O'Reilly was a bishop. Perhaps it was at that time he did publish,
in the sense of printing, one of the catechisms or both.

Copies of the English texts are rare. There is not one to be found
in the National Library. Copies from the latest printings are even
difficult to come by. The oldest copies I have discovered are in
the library of the British Museum, a printing by N. Greacen of
Monaghan, tentatively dated 1819, and an 1825 printing also from
Monaghan by Charles Gass. The Franciscan Library in Killiney
has a Dublin printing by Richard Grace and there is one by Simms
and McIntyre of Belfast in Thurles College, both dated 1826.

37

Maynooth College has copies of a C. M. Warren printing, undated, which may be placed c. 1860. James Duffy & Co., then operating from 38 Westmoreland Street, Dublin, were responsible for the printings that saw the catechism out. I have a copy from what I believe is the final reprint, dated 1949.

The fidelity of the tradition one comes to regard as predictable emerges loud and clear from a study of these texts; they are almost word for word the same. Richard Grace elects for the more dynamic Abridgment *of Faith* on his title page in contrast to Abridgment *of the Christian Doctrine* in the Duffy printing. You have to search closely to find a variant in the text, *dues* for *tithes*, for instance or a change that had to be made in the O'Hussey style rhymed version of the Church commandments to keep up with the law, this done very neatly, 'And on all Fridays flesh thou shalt not taste' replacing 'Fridays and Saturdays flesh thou shalt not taste'. The couplets, a pleasant break in the somewhat stilted exposition of right and wrong, occur in all the printings. By poetic licence they make eight Church precepts out of the usual six:

    I. Sundays and holidays Mass thou shalt hear.
    II. And holidays sanctify through all the year.
    III. Lent and Ember days, and vigils thou shalt fast.
    IV. Fridays and Saturdays flesh thou shalt not taste.
    V. In Lent and Advent nuptial feasts forbear.
    VI. Confess your sins at least once every year.
    VII. Receive your God about great Easter-day.
    VIII. And to his Church neglect not tithes to pay.

The Acts of Contrition, Faith, Hope and Charity, together with the Prayer before the Acts, that used to be recited in our churches before the principal Mass are given in the Duffy printing only. The Prayer before Mass that went along with the Acts in our liturgy for so long is curiously omitted. These prayers are later than O'Reilly's time, although the tradition of reciting acts of these virtues is not and examples are found in O'Reilly texts both in Irish and in English. In the O'Reilly catechisms as in others a note accompanying the 'Acts' recommends the devotion especially at morning and evening prayer and before confession and communion and draws attention to the indulgence granted by Pope Clement XIV on 5 April 1772 to Irish Catholics who practise it. The O'Reilly 'Acts' are not meant for recitation before Mass; indeed the Act of Faith although cast in prayer form would replace his catechetical *Abridgment*. Examples of these 'Acts', sharing the introductory prayer with O'Reilly but otherwise considerably different from his, are to be found in the original Butler catechisms,

38

both Irish and English, and in the so-called Plunket catechism of Meath printed by Gill where they appear also in both languages. It seems reasonable to suppose that these prayers are the work, not necessarily original, of Archbishop Butler. They appear again in emended form, but no doubting the source, in the Duffy O'Reilly.

The emended 'Long Acts' with the accompanying Prayer before Mass were first prescribed by the Provincial Synod of Thurles in 1810. They are included in the proceedings of the Synod published by Fitzpatrick of Dublin in 1813 along with a note from Archbishop Bray, Butler's successor as Archbishop of Cashel, ordering that they should be read together with the Angelus before Mass on all Sundays and holidays.[1] The suggestion by the Meath historian, John Brady, that Butler is the author of the 'Acts' in their emended form and of the Prayer before Mass is based on his assumption that Butler also wrote the 'General Catechism' that bears his name, which of course he did not.[2] The rhythm of the prayers is certainly that of the 'General' and the plea in the Prayer before Mass 'for all that are in high station, that we may lead quiet and holy lives' has the political undertones of that text. The prayers were prescribed by the Provincial Synod of Dublin in 1831 and they spread in time throughout the whole country.[3] They have come down to us like so much of the catechism texts word for word perfect.

It has been said of the emended versions to which Irish ears were attuned for nearly a century and a half that 'they write themselves upon the memory like music'.[4] They do indeed; from the introductory Prayer before the Acts to the end of the especially sonorous Prayer before Mass, every one of them is rich in that quality the Latin sentence is able to bestow on a declamation.

O my God: who hast graciously promised every blessing, even heaven itself, through Jesus Christ, to those who keep Thy commandments; relying on Thy infinite power, goodness and mercy, and on Thy sacred promises to which Thou art always faithful, I confidently hope to obtain pardon of all my sins, grace to serve Thee faithfully in this life, by doing the good works Thou hast commanded, and which, with Thy assistance, I now purpose to perform, and eternal happiness in the next, through my Lord and Saviour Jesus Christ.

1 See article by Aodh de Blacam in *The Irish Monthly*, September 1940.
2 'The Prayers before Mass on Sundays and Holydays in Ireland' in *I.E.R.*, August 1947.
3 de Blacam, op. cit.
4 de Blacam, op. cit.

There is another throw forward to Butler within the catechism text itself occuring this time in all the surviving English printings. The lesson on the Sacrifice of the Mass, just before the chapters on sin at the end of Part II, is a word for word repeat of Lesson XXXIII from the original Butler catechism. The lesson is completely out of context in the O'Reilly text and there is nothing whatever to suggest that Butler might have borrowed from O'Reilly; actually a lesson on the Mass — *Do'n Aifrionn Neevha* — in question and answer form is printed in the Ulster Irish texts, as a kind of after-thought, isolated from the catechism proper at the end of the booklet.

The Duffy O'Reilly catechism was used in the diocese of Clogher to the 1950s when catechisms throughout the country were gradually replaced by the national text. By this time, however, the catechism as such was tending to become little more than a basis for an elaborate programme of religious instruction, rather like tables and the five finger exercises in the teaching of arithmetic and the piano. Doctrine, in the sense of instruction, was given its own slot on the syllabus, the subject prescribed often having no relation to the corresponding catechism lesson. This was the system followed in Clogher. According to the syllabus for the late 1940s the (then surviving) Standards VII and VIII were to repeat all four parts of O'Reilly as a kind of grand finale, and the pupils were also expected to have read either Power's *Manual of Religious Instruction* or the Christian Brothers' *Companion to the Catechism*, explanatory texts that were beamed on the Maynooth Catechism in the Butler tradition.[5] There was a lot of temperance instruction with emphasis on drunkenness and total abstinence. The prayer schedule was brought into line with contemporary devotions. Provision for prayers in Irish and for some Irish catechism, a few chapters from the Raphoe text, as a kind of gesture then common to many parts of the country, and there was a course of Bible history for all grades that would have been very much a work of supererogation for many years after O'Reilly's day. The syllabus entirely ignored the *Abridgment of Faith* and more singularly the *Confirmation Catechism*. No doubt at the time, as in so much of the North, the children were confirmed from the age of seven in accordance with the canon law. But what this distinguished catechism would have meant to older boys and girls! Give them a teacher of any imagination and how they would have felt the poignancy of O'Reilly's predicament and been stirred by his

5 Religious Examination of Catholic Schools in the Diocese of Clogher, *Annual Report, 1945*, Omagh: The North West of Ireland Printing and Publishing Company, pp. 22-24.

40

eloquence.

One presumes that the diocese of Derry, O'Reilly's first episcopal home, remained consistently loyal to his catechism. At any rate the text in use for more than fifty years before the end was O'Reilly's in a 'New Edition, Revised and enlarged with the approbation of the Most Rev. Dr. O'Doherty'. It bears the *imprimatur* of Bishop John K. O'Doherty of Derry, dated July 1897, and was printed in Derry by the Derry Journal Office, 8vo., pp. 64, in that year. I take it that the copy in my possession comes from a re-issue; I remember getting it with some difficulty, second hand, in the later 1950s; it once belonged to Nancy Davidson.

Nancy and her companions were fortunate. The Derry O'Reilly is without any doubt the best religion booklet of its class we had in our schools. I say booklet rather than catechism because it really was a manual of religion and piety, a Catechism Prayer Book, more space devoted to prayers, instructions and pious exercises than to the formal questions and answers. It is well laid out and printed on good paper. St Peter Canisius would no doubt have enlivened the text with wood-cuts, but I feel he would have liked it.

The catechism is run through in thirty-seven lessons, but the O'Reilly structure is there, the four parts, and the text is more enlarged than revised. There is some useful reconstruction. Sin is treated more properly within the Creed, with its appropriate article, and the lesson on the Mass, the one repeated from Butler, comes in the section on the sacraments where the Holy Eucharist is seen as both sacrifice and sacrament. Certain *lacunae* in the original text are filled in; O'Reilly had nothing to say about things like purgatory or indulgences which were not inconsequent in his time. Provision is made also for doctrinal definitions after O'Reilly's time, the doctrines of the Immaculate Conception of Our Lady and Papal Infallibility.

The *Abridgment of Faith* and the *Confirmation Catechism* were regretably omitted but the extensive collection of prayers and devotions is a valuable survival for the Tridentine museum; it gets together so much of the prayer life and piety of our people in the later years of the era. O'Reilly's schedule of morning and evening prayers is there, complete with the meditative pauses. Pious practices unknown to O'Reilly's people are there also in the rich profusion we knew them in our time — the Way of the Cross, Devotions to the Sacred Heart, the Benediction, Devotion to Our Lady of Good Counsel, the October Devotions with Leo XIII's Prayer to St Joseph, 'To thee, O Blessed Joseph we have recourse in our tribulations ...'. The practice of ejaculatory prayer, in some measure replacing the sombre meditations of O'Reilly's time, is

41

well provided for. Simple, unsophisticated religion:

What should you do when the devil tempts you with bad thoughts?
Pray, 'Jesus and Mary help me'.

A long list of aspirations, all indulgenced, taken from *The Raccolta*.[6] Prayers for special occasions, with the recurring enticement of an indulgence, often applicable to the souls in purgatory, when tempted, for the faithful in their agony, before and after meals, for a happy death, whilst dressing. Childhood jingles:

Jesus meek and Jesus mild,
Pity me a little child.
Jesus, take my heart and bless it,
That nothing evil may possess it.

This from *The Raccolta*, reflecting a widespread devotion, often repeated throughout a lifetime:

Angel of God, my guardian dear,
To whom His love commits me here,
Ever this day be at my side,
To light and guard, to rule and guide.

Angele Dei, qui custos es mei, me tibi commissum
pietate superna hodie illumina, custodi, rege et
guberna.

A selection is included of the more popular formal prayers, the Memorare, the prayer of St Ignatius ('Soul of Christ, sanctify me ...') the prayer called *En Ego* from the introductory words of the Latin form, to be recited before a crucifix 'after receiving'; and a script on Blessed Objects (the scapulars, brown and blue, holy water, blessed medals) encouraged as praiseworthy habits. The form of confession is given with apppropriate instruction in catechetical form, how to prepare, how to confess and how to clinch the exercise with fruitful resolution of sinning no more. This exercise, detached from the catechism proper, and so beamed on spiritual effort, goes to emphasise the Tridentine preoccupation with sin as an offence against God, the heart reaching towards 'sorrow for having offended God, *Who is infinitely good in Himself*, or for having pained our Divine Lord', the renewal of sorrow at

6 *The Raccolta or Prayers and Devotions Enriched with Indulgences*, edited and in part newly translated into English from the 1938 official edition *Preces et Pia Opera* issued by the Sacred Penitentiary Apostolic and with later additions, New York, 1943.

the foot of the Cross, thinking of the Saviour and 'how much my sins have wounded Him', and finally the down to earth business of keeping straight:

You have four things to do after confession — 1. Go to some quiet place, kneel down again, and thank God for his great mercy to you. 2. Say your penance, or part of it, exactly and piously. 3. Renew your resolution to keep away from all sin, and all the persons, places, or things that drew you into sin. 4. Beg God's grace to keep this resolution faithfully.

A feature of so many of our catechisms was an outline of the manner of serving a priest at Mass, sometimes as here with detailed instruction on how the actions are performed.

P. Introibo ad altare Dei.
C. Ad Deum qui laetificat juventutem meam.

'I will go to the altar of God, to the God who giveth joy to my youth ...' Already before the priest had gone to the altar at the principal Masses he would have recited the 'Acts', facing the people, reading from a chart. They are here, convenient, too, in the Derry O'Reilly, along with the Prayer before Mass. Even the Leonine Prayers are provided in this collection, those ordered by Leo XIII, the last lingering echo in our memories of the Tridentine Mass:

O God, our refuge and our strength, look down with favour on Thy people who cry to Thee; and through the intercession of the glorious and Immaculate Vigin Mary Mother of God, of Saint Joseph, her Spouse, of Thy holy Apostles Peter and Paul, and all Thy Saints, in mercy and goodness hear our prayers for the conversion of sinners, and for the liberty and exaltation of our Holy Mother the Church. Through Christ our Lord. Amen.

Blessed Michael, Archangel, defend us in the hour of conflict; be our safeguard against the wickedness and snares of the devil — may God restrain him, we humbly pray, and do thou, O Prince of the Heavenly Host, by the power of God, thrust Satan down to hell, and with him the other wicked spirits who wander through the world for the ruin of souls. Amen.

A programme of religious instruction for the diocese of Derry is added to this interesting textbook, the usual compartmental structure of prayers, catechism, doctrine and history. The accompanying notes — 1897 — illuminate our catechetical history in a manner analogous to O'Reilly's preamble to his Confirmation text. Teachers are advised that when Religious Instruction happens to be immediately before or after school hours, Rule 87 of the Commissioners permits the Angelus to be said at mid-day, and there is now no objection, on the part of the Board, to the display in the schoolroom at all times of *pictures* illustrative of events recorded in sacred scripture, such as The Annunciation, The Visitation, The Nativity, The Crucifixion, Christ Blessing Children. Statues apparently were still banned.

Raphoe was the third of the three Northern dioceses to carry the O'Reilly tradition to our time. The text in use there for the last forty years of the era was the 'Catechism of Christian Doctrine, Approved for the Diocese of Raphoe'; my copy from the Fifth Edition, Letterkenny: The County Donegal Printing Company Ltd, 8vo, pp. 72. O'Reilly's name is omitted from the title page, but despite considerable emendation the text is unmistakeably his. Father Philip O'Boyle who had been Diocesan Inspector of Schools in the Raphoe diocese and subsequently became parish priest of Termon, Co. Donegal, sent me this account in 1951 of the origin of the catechism.

The author of the Raphoe Catechism was Reverend Joseph O'Boyle, a native of Creeslough who was ordained in 1892 in Maynooth and died at Christmas in 1920. He was the first Diocesan Inspector, appointed in 1903 and held the position until he was appointed P.P. here in Termon in 1915; in 1917 he was transferred to Carrigart where he was 'till his death. He was a distinguished theologian, regarded by the priests as *episcopabilis*, but his health was poor and he died young. I think the catechism was first published in 1910 ....

In fact the publication date was somewhat later because the catechism quotes from the decree *Quam Singulari* of the Sacred Congregation of the Sacraments, dated 10 August 1910, bearing on the age for admission to first communion, and the text is constructed with an eye to the new discipline. Two catechisms are supplied, one for the first communion class and the other for those already admitted. The second part is complementary to the first, with no repetition.

Quam Singulari marked the Church's formal recognition of the newly developing child psychology and of fresh insights to the education of the young; it was a children's charter of rights to responsible sacramental life from the dawn of reason. The Raphoe revision of O'Reilly was our first step towards a child-centred catechesis, a tiny faltering step but it was taken. The first communion catechism consists of the early lessons of O'Reilly's in O'Reilly's words, almost unaltered, with a few original lessons on commandments, confession and communion, eight lessons in

44

PRAYER WHILST DRESSING.

O God clothe my soul with a nuptial robe of charity, and grant that I may wear it pure and undefiled before Thy judgment seat.

GRACE BEFORE MEALS.

Bless yourself and say :

Bless us, O Lord, and these Thy gifts which of Thy bounty we are about to receive ; through Christ our Lord. Amen.

GRACE AFTER MEALS.

We give Thee thanks, O Lord, for these and all Thy other gifts, which of Thy bounty we have received, through Christ our Lord. Amen.

May the divine assistance remain always with us, and may the souls of the faithful departed, through the mercy of God, rest in peace. Amen.

INDULGENCED ASPIRATIONS.

(Taken from the Raccolta).

My Jesus, mercy.

Praised be the Holy Name of Jesus for ever and ever. Amen.

Jesus, my God, I love Thee above all things.

Praised, blessed, adored, and loved be Jesus Christ in the most Holy Sacrament of the Altar in every Tabernacle throughout the world.

O Sacrament most holy, O Sacrament Divine,

All praise and all thanksgiving be every moment Thine.

O Sweetest Heart of Jesus, I implore,

That I may daily love Thee more and more.

May the Sacred Heart of Jesus be everywhere loved.

Jesus, meek and humble of heart, make my heart like unto Thine.

Sweet Heart of Jesus, be Thou my love. *(300 days' Indulgence every time).*

Sweet Heart of Mary, be my salvation. *(300 days' Indulgence every time).*

O Eternal Father, I offer Thee the Precious Blood of Jesus Christ in atonement for all my sins, and for the wants of our Holy Mother the Church.

May the most just, most high, and most amiable will of God be in all things done, praised, and for ever magnified.

Come, O Holy Ghost, enlighten the minds of all and fill our hearts with Thy Love.

Mary, conceived without sin, pray for us who have recourse to thee.

Praised be the Holy and Immaculate Conception of Mary ever a Virgin.

Mary, through thy pure and Immaculate Conception obtain for me purity of body and sanctity of soul.

St. Joseph, friend of the Sacred Heart, pray for us.

Blessed be the Holy and Undivided Trinity now and for ever. Amen

Page from an 1897 Derry edition of the O'Reilly Catechism

Lesson VII.—THE POPE.

1—Who is the Pope ?

The Pope is the visible head of the Church, successor of St. Peter, and vicar of Jesus Christ on earth.

2—Who g

Jesus Ch
to St.
(John

3—What
is Inf

I mean t
shephe
defines
to be b

1—*Pope.* The w
  can be seen.

Successor of St
  and authori
  the Pope is

Vicar of Chris
  and takes H

3—*Infallible.* F

Define. To se
  mean teachi
  a doctrine a

Faith or mora
  we are to do

Lesson VIII.

COMMUNION OF SAINTS. PURGATORY.

1—What do you understand by the Communion of Saints ?

I understand that the members of the Church form one body in Jesus Christ, and have a share in the same spiritual benefits.

2—What are these spiritual benefits in which members of the Church share ?

They are the Sacraments, the holy sacrifice of the Mass, the prayers of the Church, and the good works of the just.

3—Who are deprived of these spiritual advantages ?

Infidels, Heretics, Schismatics, and Excommunicated persons.

4—What is Purgatory ?

Purgatory is a state or place of punishment in the next life where some souls suffer for a time on account of their sins.

5—Who go to Purgatory ?

Those who die in venial sin, and those who have not fully paid the debt of temporal punishment due for sins already forgiven.

27

Pages from a 1925 printing (fifth edition) of the Raphoe O'Reilly Catechism all, some fifty formulas. The moral instruction is not above the children's heads:

Q. Mention some of the things the Commandments tell us to do?

A. They tell us to say our prayers, to go to Mass on Sundays, to obey our parents and to speak the truth always.

Q. Mention some of the things the Commandments forbid us to do?

A. They forbid us to curse or say bad words, to strike or quarrel with others, to be immodest or to tell lies.

There was not of course the slightest hint of what the new education was going to mean for the teaching of the faith in Montessori's 'century of the child'.[7] The broad theological and moral concepts were still presented as if to adults. The children were told they must confess their mortal sins without exception and that without confession not one of those sins would be forgiven. They are gravely warned against concealing a mortal sin. Venial sins are mentioned casually; they are not bound to confess them but it is very useful to do so.

The catechism for the older children has O'Reilly's four parts and is spread over 41 lessons including a 'Christian Rule of Life' after the manner of the English 'penny' catechism and ending with a temperance lesson. In section two, on the commandments, before the study of the moral law proper, there is a little chapter on 'Charity' following the recitation of the decalogue and the reduction of the ten to the two laws of love. This rectifies O'Reilly's blunder which found him at the end of his instruction with *caritas* on his hands, undefined, and wondering what to do with it. The point is no mere detail, because the whole idea of the Canisian structure is to ensure that the catechism is suffused by the theological virtues of faith, hope and charity, and in particular to show how obedience to the commandments is the only real proof of a love of God and neighbour that is rooted in our faith and hope.

Unfortunately O'Reilly's ploy of calling for the exercise of the virtue in act once it is defined is abandoned. Indeed the catechism becomes more and more technical. It is peppered with those 'Catechism Notes', elaborations on the text that became so popular in the later years of the era; they appear at the foot of every lesson in the smallest print, building up more and more to knowledge but diverting from the force and the shock of O'Reilly's rudimentary themes. The emended wording was a help no doubt, but one cannot help wondering if the simplification of that sort

7 Maria Montessori, *The Secret of Childhood*, London, 1936, pp. 3f.

of catechism could ever be really a success. O'Reilly's language was archaic and earthy as time went by; it belonged to an age, but it had life and strength, it was his greatest asset. The 'smutty discourses' and 'lewd kisses' of the original must have appeared crude to an age that had become increasingly reticent and even prim; the revision elected for 'all words, looks and actions contrary to holy purity'. O'Reilly's delicate perception of the husband and wife relationship was lost also; the memorable formulas, which Donlevy was to repeat, are left out.

The *Abridgment of Faith* and the *Confirmation Catechism* are not given, nor is O'Reilly's prayer schedule for morning and evening. The later vintage of Tridentine devotion is borrowed from the Derry Catechism. The Latin hymns for Benediction of the Most Blessed Sacrament are given, the only hymns I have noticed in the O'Reilly catechisms. The Tridentine Mass is there, all set up for the altar boys.

5

The Irish texts

As already noted, copies from the printings of the catechism in Irish have survived in abundance. In the likely places one looks they pop up not only in single files but in battalions: in the National Library, the British Museum, Maynooth, in the Bradshaw Collection of the University of Cambridge, the Franciscan Library Killiney, University College Cork, the Cork City Library, and in that 'outstanding American institution', as President Kennedy called it, the Library of Congress. There are copies of printings in every decade from the 1770's to the 1860's. I have found nothing from the two following decades, but in the wake of the language revival that was stepping up towards the end of the century there are printings in 1891 and 1901, and the Irish O'Reilly was there in use at the end in the version emended by Father Joseph O'Boyle for the diocese of Raphoe. The popularity of the catechism in Munster was of course a factor in this happy survival; there were a lot of them there for the picking. But the main factor was the zeal of the Irish language enthusiasts who had been consistently garnering the little books for linguistic purposes; a printing by Warren of Dublin is listed in the *National Union Catalog (Pre-1956 Imprints)* as bound with *An Cheud Leabhar Gaedilge*, a little work by the Society for the Preservation of the Irish Language dated 1882.

The linguists had a busy time correcting mistakes. The texts are uniformly poor, produced by printers who had apparently no knowledge of Irish. Not indeed that a reading knowledge of the language would have been of such help because the vast majority of the texts use phonetic spelling. Only a couple of the Munster printings use the *Cló Romhánach* proper, and O'Reilly's catechism did not appear in Gaelic script until 1863, in the William Williams' revision.

The oldest text in Ulster Irish which I have traced is in the British Museum, printed in 1793 by Joseph Parks of Dundalk, *An Teagask Creestye agus Paidreagha na Mainne agus an Tranona*, 12mo, pp. 48. There is no mention of O'Reilly on the title page. Subsequent printings are faithful transcripts. They repeat the mistakes or make fresh ones of their own, as no doubt Parks had already done in his turn. N. Greacen of Monaghan, in the area that was to prove so faithful to the O'Reilly tradition, had an updated printing which the catalogues place about 1819. There must of course have been others in the North, but most of the surviving copies come from the Dublin presses that looked after the Catholic cause in that age of controversial religious printing: J. Dunn, 1800; P. Wogan, 1802; R. Cross, 1808; W. Jones, 1814; D. Wogan, 1820; R. Grace, 1826; Caleb Connolly, 1833; G.P. Warren, 1854; and about that time, C. M. Warren, whose productions were usually undated.

The Irish texts differ little from the English. The lay-out is the same, with the same tendency to carelessness about headings; the name of a part, *An Ran*, will be left out and the title of a lesson frequently missed. The construction and arrangement of the text is slightly different. Here and there the matter composing a single formula in the English is broken into two or three to suit the Irish. Occasionally the Irish text will have an additional formula by way of introduction or expansion of the theme. This additional material when repeated by Donlevy would seem to establish the Irish version as the older of the two. Some examples will illustrate what little difference there is between the two versions and, of more interest perhaps, will serve to highlight the curiosity of a phonetic catechism.

In the third lesson of the first part, the probing of the mystery of the Trinity, effected in a single formula in the English, requires three in the Irish:

K. Ke occa is sinne, no is oge?

F. Is inan aois, uaisle, agus onoir yaav.

K. Ke occa is far, an Tahir, an Mak, no an Spirid neev?

F. Is inan feous, agus maihis yaav.

K. Ke occa is luahie hanic air an teel?

F. Ta siad an on teeryact rive nulle heel.

An instance of this sort of expansion, for controversial reasons, occurs in the lesson following. In place of the English, 'What is He called since He became man? He is called Jesus Christ', two questions are put, the second repeated by Donlevy.

K. Ke occa is far Iosa Kreesta, na a Mahir?

F. Is far Iosa Kreesta, do vri gur far Dia no duinne, cruhior no cretuir.

K. Ke he Iosa Kreesta?

48

F. An dara parsa don Trinoid neefa ylak colan deena.

In several places one notes a formula extra to the English text which happens to be repeated by Donlevy. This one, significantly, in the lesson on the Church:

K. An riachtanach do yunne ve san eglish an a ve savalta?

F. Is riachtanach, do vri nach wil slainte le fail amuy as a neglish.

In the fifth lesson of the second part, the notable admonition to husband and wife comes with a prefatory enquiry by way of call to duty:

K. An Loran an ahnese air yualgus a nir heev a vna posta, no na mna heev a fir?

F. Lory gan avras.

I find two other examples. In the lesson on sin, the admonition to avoid it as 'the greatest of all evils' is clinched with this argument:

K. Gud ime shin?

F. Do vri gur be an paku a wain a ni nawid do Yia yeen, agus yamnees go sheery shin.

And in Lesson 3 of the fourth part, on good works, the matter of the English second lesson — a slight difference in the arrangement of the lesson material here — there is an introductory formula:

K. Ka veud kineul deaghoibre ann?

F. An tri go prinsapalta, urny, trosgu and deirk.

On the other hand, there are some additions and slants in the Irish text that one suspects reflect an extra stern O'Reilly; perhaps he had mellowed by the time he came to writing in English! Donlevy does not repeat. This question with its doleful and unduly dogmatic answer rounds off the text on the fifth commandment:

K. An paku run deeltish agus uilk?

F. Is paku marfave, agus ta moran a nifrin fan run shin, mar fuair baas gan feesidin agus ahri yenu an.

'Ta moran a nifrin'. This tendency to multiply the heads in hell was certainly a characteristic of our Tridentine moral instruction. Three times, O'Reilly repeats the grim warning, they are going to hell in no small numbers because they died in their sins without confession or penance.

The catechism is followed by the *Abridgment of Faith* — AHYIRRA *an chredi is koir a leu don phobal De-dony* — headed just like that — and by the after-thought lesson on the holy Mass mentioned already, *Do'n Aifrionn Neevha*. The confirmation Catechism is not in these texts; I cannot recall having found it except in a modified form in some of the Munster O'Reilly's. Neither is the Mass serving exercise. The Mass lesson is repeated word for word in Donlevy's Lesson 8 of his fourth part, 'Of the Holy Mass, and of the Manner of hearing it'. O'Reilly closes his lesson with prayers, found also in Donlevy, which are to be said as the Host and the Chalice are elevated.

Oraid is feidir do yenu le togvail Choirp Chriosd

A Hierna, credim go deivin go vuil Thu idir Fhuil agus Fheoil, idir Anum fos agus Diachta go firinach an se Tacramintse Ayraim agus molaim Hu innte, o mo croiye go hiomlan.

Oraid le togvail na Chailisi

A Hierna, ayraim de Huil ior-usal; do verim mile beacas Yuit fa na dortav air mo hon a grann na Croiche. Na leig yau a torav do chailleav, tre mo pheacaive.

Donlevy repeats the prayers within his text, the English version as follows:

Q. What do you at the Elevation of the *Blessed Host*, that is, the *Body of Christ*?

A. I say: O Lord, I verily believe, that thy Body and Blood, thy Soul and Divinity also, are really present in this Sacrament. I do with all my heart adore and praise thee therein.

Q. What do you say at the Elevation of the *Chalice*?

A. I say: O Lord, I adore thy most Precious Blood: I give thee infinite Thanks for having shed it for my sake on the Cross. Suffer me not, by my Sins, to lose the Fruit thereof.

The *Paidreagha* are printed before the catechism text; in the Parks edition they occupy fourteen pages, a proportion of the whole exercise suggested by the title page. These prayers and devotions were securely built into Irish piety in the 18th century and remained the pith of it for a considerable part of the century following. A popular devotional work, *The Spiritual Rose*, a method of saying the rosaries of the Most Holy Name of Jesus and the Blessed Virgin, with their litanies, together with meditations and prayers adapted to the Holy Way of the Cross, was translated into

50

Irish and printed in Monaghan in 1800, twice in 1819 and again in 1825 and 1835.[1] The 1835 edition — the translator was Mathew Kennedy and the printer Greacen — contains Irish religious verse by Rev. Bernard Callan and the *Paidreagha na Mainne* of the catechism.

The Munster texts really do abound. The oldest I have seen are from Cork and Limerick. The Cork text, to my knowledge the oldest surviving O'Reilly catechism, is *An Teagasg Cristuy; agus U'rnihe na Mainne, agus an Trahno'na*, 'Ar na chur anglo le Doncha O Donnoghue, Ag Corca, M. DCC, LXXIV', in phonetic spelling, 12mo, pp. 58. The morning and evening devotions begin with prayers to the Holy Spirit from the Roman Missal. The prayer sequences show some variations by comparison with the Ulster texts we have been considering, especially in the forms of the 'Acts', but substantially they are the same with the emphasis on devotion to the persons of Jesus and Mary and centred on the respective litanies. After the catechism proper comes the special Confirmation text, the same structure as the English version but in less detail and without the interesting introduction. The *Ahgearra an Crediv* follows, then a form of the 'Acts' in English and 'The Manner of Serving Mass' with directives to the server in English also. The supplementary lesson on the Mass, *Do'n Aifrionn Neevha*, is omitted; whatever Poor Scholar may have brought the catechism to Munster must have used a text without it, you never find it in the Munster printings. With only a few minor exceptions the catechism itself tallies with the Ulster text. The Twelve Fruits of the Holy Spirit, for example, omitted no doubt by traditional error from the seventh lesson of the first part in the Ulster texts, are recited here as they are in the English catechism. The first lesson of *An 3 Rann* shows some differences. The question *Ce as Christuy ann?* appears, as in the English version, *What is a Christian?*, and with the same answer in abbreviated form. A definition of Confirmation follows, somewhat more elaborate than the one supplied in the Ulster texts; then two formulas, not in the Ulster Irish nor in our English versions, covering the further effects of confirmation and the fuller influence of the Holy Ghost's visit in this sacrament than in baptism. These formulas are based on Lesson II of the Confirmation Catechism. Another of these quite insignificant variations occurs in the very first lesson, *An Ched Cheacht*, the four things to be done, determining the now familiar structure of the catechism, being gathered into a single *Fregra* which, repeated precisely as it is

1 See note entered by Séamus Ó Casaide on the copy of the 1835 edition in Maynooth College Library.

printed, offers a fair sample of the only sort of religious instruction in this category that could have been of any benefit to so many of our forbears of that age:

An che'd ni, Gach ni doilsig Dia, agus do vuinas an Eagluis du'in, do chrediov go dingva'lta; an tara ni, ahanta De agus na heagluise do cho'vlina; an treas ni, Na Sacraminti do ghlaca leis an oliu' riachtanach. An Cearhu' ni, Dochus do chur an Dia agus trial air go minick leis na hu'rnihe.

The Limerick text, *Teagask Creestye agus Paidreagha na Maine agus an Tranona*, was printed by W. Goggin, described on the title-page as Bookseller and Stationer, Corner of Bridge-street, Formerly Quay-Lane. No date is given but the catalogue of the Bradshaw Collection of the University of Cambridge, which holds a copy, suggests the 1780's.[2] The Cambridge copy stops at p. 24, towards the end of *An 9 Ceacht* of the first part, but thus far, the variation of title notwithstanding, it corresponds in every particular with Doncha O'Donnoghue's printing. Professor Brendán Ó Madagáin compared it with an 1819 printing by J. Geary of Cork, claiming to be the Fourth Edition (copy in the Killiney Franciscan Library) and found the two texts word for word the same.[3]

This predictable reiteration down to the mistakes is the stamp of the minor riot of O'Reilly printings in Munster throughout the first half of the nineteenth century. Cork printers were the most prolific; Geary, Mulcahy, Dillon, O'Rourke from the city; J. Lindsey and Brothers from Fermoy. John O'Rourke and D. Mulcahy issued the catechism as late as 1862 and even after the William Williams revision C. Diolun did a printing in 1864; there is a copy in the Cork City Library. The O'Rourke and Mulcahy printings together with an undated C. M. Warren edition issued about the same time come in Roman type but not phonetically spelt. The title of these versions, *An Teagusg Críosduighe do reir Ceist agus Treagradh*, suggests that the printers were no more skilled than were their predecessors in Gaelic orthography. Moreover, they made an error peculiar to themselves in attributing the origin of the catechism to Archbishop Butler of Cashel — 'Aistrighioghe ogh Leabhair Teagusg Easpoig Bullair, Ardeispoig Caeshiol'. There was in fact in circulation at the time a Butler text in Irish said to have been a translation of an English original by Bishop Coppinger. This misapplication of authorship on the title pages

2 See Brendán Ó Madagáin, *An Gaelige i Luimneach 1700-1900*, Baile Átha Cliath: An Clochomhar Tta, 1974, foot-note 90, p. 42. According to R. Herbert's *Limerick Printers and Printing*, 1942, Goggin was in business in Limerick from 1784 to 1809.

3 Ó Madagáin, loc. cit.

of our catechisms had a consistency of its own somewhat comparable to the fidelity with which the texts were transmitted.[4] The Munster O'Reilly in this new garb was passed faithfully on. I have compared the O'Rourke, Mulcahy and Warren *Teagusg Críosduighe* with the Doncha O'Donnoghue printing and find their versions tally exactly; the only difference in the booklets other than the orthographic one worth noting is the omission of the 'Acts' in English and the Mass Serving printed by O'Donnoghue after the *Ahgearra an Crediv.*

By the 1860's phonetical catechetical instruction in Irish was a thing of the past. The O'Rourke and Mulcahy O'Reilly's of 1862, which one could learn to read as well as to recite, were still of course employed for teaching the faith, but they were used also, despite the defects, as a source material for the study of the language and its orthography. William Williams of Dungarvan, the Keating Society's editor of the revised version of the catechism, was quite frank about this. The Williams' O'Reilly was published in Dublin in 1863 by Seon F. Fobhlaeir in two editions, one in Gaelic and the other in Roman characters. In his Preface dated Feast of St Patrick, Apostle of Ireland, 1863, from Dungarvan, Williams relates the circumstances in which the new printing was undertaken and its function as understood in the framework of the Irish revival. The catechism, 'having passed through numerous editions in the hands of printers unacquainted with the language; was found to be so filled with errors as to be of little practical use. The first intention was to bring out a corrected version, but Bishop Moriarty of Kerry suggested that the work be enlarged so as to make it 'complete as an elementary catechism'. Williams extols the superiority of Irish over English as a medium of religious instruction, quoting the late bishop of his diocese, Dr Abraham, to this effect, the one who declared that the children he met on his Confirmation rounds who were taught their catechism in Irish surpassed those taught it in English 'as the rational being surpassed in solid sense the chattering jay'! But for Williams the exercise was not by any means wholly catechetical. He puts in a word for the use of the catechism as an instrument for teaching Irish. He saw it as 'a class-book in the hands of many thousands who, throughout the province, are now learning to read and write the olden tongue'.

The revision was launched with the sanction of the Archbishop and Bishops of Munster:

4 In the *National Union Catalog, Pre-1956 Imprints,* two O'Reilly Munster texts are attributed to Archbishop Butler: *An Teagasg Cristuy agus Urnithe an Mainne agus na Trahnona,* Fermoy: J. Lindsey and Bros. 18- ; and Cork: C. Dillon, 1838.

An Teagasg Críostuidhe, Agus na Gnáth-Urnaighthe, Nuadh-Scríobhtha agus Léir-Cheartuighthe, le Fuirionn Dhoctúir Ceitin, Re H-Aonta Aird-Easpuig Caisil agus Imligh, agus na N-Easpog uile Chúigidh Mumhan.

Episcopal letters of approbation are reproduced, and it is interesting to find Bishop Moriarty referring to it as the new edition of 'the Irish Catechism', not as implying that it was the only Irish text available but simply as a generic term covering any catechism in the Irish language; Butler used the same phrase in reference to the Gaelic version of his famous text.

Before the catechism begins there is a short instruction on the language itself, such as Donlevy and other Irish-catechism makers provided, the sounds of the vowels, diphthongs, triphthongs, consonants and the like. The text is based on the Munster printings we have been considering. The lay-out is very good, Williams proved an excellent editor, the parts and lessons all carefully titled, the *Aithgearra* suitably paragraphed and sub-headed. The Confirmation Catechism is there complete and the usual Manner of Serving Mass. The Gaelic script is very attractive, the print throughout a pleasing size. The Council of the Keating Society did O'Reilly proud.

It is not difficult to trace the source of the additions the editor decided on, following Bishop Moriarty's advice. The title page carries the two scripture texts, Mc.10:14 and Jn.17:3, that appear on so many Butler catechisms. Butler's 'General', then in such wide possession, was bound to be an influence and so it proved. The other text that helped was the 'Short Donlevy', as I have called it, the Tuam catechism of Martin Loftus which we will be meeting later. The questions on the marks of the true Church inserted in *An 8 Ceacht* of the first *Rann* are from the 'General', and the additional instruction on the nature of oaths and vows etc. in *An 3 Ceacht* of the second *Rann* comes from the same source. The Tuam catechism supplies the six additional formulas in the first lesson of the third part, turning on the distinction of the sacraments into those of the living and those of the dead, those that can be received once only and the necessity of having a *meas mór* for the sacraments in general. The Tuam is the source also of the six formulas on marriage law, impediments etc. added to the sixth lesson of this part.

Williams fell back on the O'Reilly texts themselves to pick and choose. The instruction on the Mass inserted in the lesson on the Blessed Eucharist (*An 5 Ceacht* of the third *Rann*) draws two of the six formulas from the *Do'n Aifrionn Neevha* of the Ulster texts. I cannot trace the source of the others.

54

Williams follows the English text in its sequence of lessons in Part IV and recites the cardinal virtues in the second lesson, omitted from the Irish versions. He gives the Confirmation Catechism in the abbreviated form of the Munster texts, and curiously perhaps he restores O'Reilly's introductory note, 'Aistrighthe o'n tSacs-Bhéarla Bhunadhasach'. It is better laid out than in the *Béarla Bunadhasach*, though apart from an exercise in translation it does not seem to have any purpose: late as 1863 a bishop keening about not being available for Confirmation and the faithful having to go without must have appeared unreal. On the other hand it was no doubt the love of the olden tongue that was uppermost in the mind of William Williams throughout the exercise.

The revision was to share the experience of those other Munster editions of having Archbishop O'Reilly deprived of his authorship. The offender this time was neither a publisher nor a printer but a cataloguer in one of the major libraries. In our National Library, the British Museum and in the Bradshaw Collection of Irish Books in the University of Cambridge, the catechism edited by Williams for the Keating Society was attributed to O'Reilly (Farrell), R.C. Bishop of Kilmore. This manifest error, manifest, I mean, to a catechetical historian, has since been corrected in the catalogues of the British Museum. Our friend, Philip O'Connell, the chronicler of Breiffne, tells us that Farrell O'Reilly, Bishop of Kilmore from 1806 to 1829, was an excellent Gaelic scholar who preached in Irish and conducted his catechetical examinations in Irish, which in his time was the everyday language of his people. Bishop Farrell's reputation, the consistent omission of Archbishop Michael's name from the title pages of the texts and of course the origin of the catechism in Kilmore must have contributed to the error. However it came to be made, O'Connell attempts to identify the source and confidently corrects the mistake from the depths of his own researches. He writes:

There is no evidence, as far as I can discover, in support of the entry in the British Museum Catalogue attributing the authorship to Bishop *Farrell* O'Reilly, nor can any authority be produced in support of it. It is most likely that the compiler of the Bradshaw collection at Cambridge merely followed the lead of the British Museum catalogue. After exhaustive enquiries I cannot find any tradition in Kilmore of Bishop Farrell having written a *Catechism*, although his powers as a linguist live in popular tradition. Such a work if published would have left some traces and I have searched in vain for a copy; hence I may state definitely that the entry in the various catalogues is merely a cataloguer's error...[5]

5 Op. cit., *The Diocese of Kilmore*, p. 536: see pp. 534-539.

The Williams' O'Reilly was reprinted in Waterford in 1901 in the wake of the Gaelic and Nationalist revival. I am not aware of any other edition. Indeed the years between were those in which the English language was ultimately consolidated and in which the British Constitution, despite the struggle of the Fenians, seemed destined to be the source of our future political and social progress. O'Reilly came to life again with the winds of change. There is an 1891 printing from the diocese of Raphoe in Gaelic script, 58 plus 10 pp., 12mo, athcliath - dubhlinne, M. H. Gill agus a Mhac: 'An Teagasg Criostaighe fa Choinne Rathaboth lé cead agus le ughdarás Easbuig no Dioghóise.' The Archbishop's name is omitted from the title page in the traditional way but the text is his, the old O'Reilly with some slight emendations.

I have compared this Raphoe edition with the Joseph Parks printing of 1793. The *Urnuighthe na Maidne* are repeated with very slight variation. To the *Urnuighthe an Tránóna* are added *An Fhaoisidin Choitchion* and the 'Acts' — *Gniomhartha Croídhe-Bhrúghaidh, Creidimh, Dóthchais agus Carthanachta* — in the later forms attributed by Brady to Butler. Added also is the Prayer before Mass from the same period, *Urnaighe le radh roimh Aifrionn*. Variation in the catechism text is similarly slight. There are some few additions. The verse form of the Ten Commandments is given in a footnote, the form in the text being the Butler version in translation. On the other hand, the verse form of the Church commandments is given as in the Parks printing with the necessary emendation to meet change of custom. The interesting additions aim at filling in what was alleged to be wanting in the original. It is to the editor's credit that so little was found. The teaching on the first commandment of the decalogue is made to touch on pit-falls awaiting minds susceptible to preternatural forces.

C. Cad eile toirmeasgthar orrainn leis an aithne so?

F. Toirmeasgthar orrainn comhairle d'irraidh air lucht- fios-dhéanadh, draoidheachta, no pisreog, no geilleadh d'orthaidhibh etc.

In the same chapter O'Reilly was found to have been unduly defensive in his treatment of the honour due in faith to Our Lady and this positive formula is added.

C. Cad e an onóir is cóir a thabhairt don' Mhaidhean Muire, Máthair Chríost?

F. Onóir ibhad ós cionn gach créatúra eile, acht neamh-chosmhúil le onóir Dé.

O'Reilly's failure, so alleged, satisfactorily to identify the nature

56

of divine grace is made up for in this nice piece of scholastic learning.

C. Cad a thuigeas tú le grásaibh Dé?

F. Tuigim na tíodhlacaidh neámhdha a dhóirteas Dia tré na mhórthrócaire féin, agus mar gheall air lóghaidheacht Iosa Críost, in ár gcroidhthibh, le ár n-glanadh ó pheacadh agus le go saoirtheachamuis an bheatha mharthanach shioruidhe.

The Mass is defined too, in that fifth lesson of the third part, entitled *On the Sacrament of the Eucharist*. The definition is from the Butler texts, and from this source also the usual Tridentine formula covering the relationship between the sacrifice of the Mass and that of the Cross.

An *Appendix* follows the catechism, some ten pages, giving the Alphabet in Irish, an explanation of ellipsis in the structure of the language and a brief Irish-English vocabulary. Nothing further. No *Abridgment of the Faith*, nor a Confirmation Catechism, nor the special lesson on the Mass, the latter deemed unnecessary on account of the insertions as quoted.

A small-size edition of this text, 48 pp., sm. 4to., titled as 'abridged', was issued by Gill in 1901.[6] The abridgment, however, consists merely in limiting the prayer section to a brief tablet, the Our Father, Hail Mary, Apostles' Creed, Confiteor etc. The text of the catechism is exactly the same as in the 1891 printing. Both texts in one binding are available in the National Library.

This Raphoe printing was not to be the last of O'Reilly on Gaelic lips. There was a version in Irish of the Raphoe catechism of Joseph O'Boyle: *An Teagasg Críostaidhe Fá Choinne Díoghóise Rátha-Bhoth, le Cead agus Ughdarás Easbuic na Díoghóise*. My copy is an undated edition from Brún agus Ó Nualláin, Teor. with the *imprimatur* of the Bishop of Raphoe, February 1929. The title-page carries the text, Mc.10:14: 'Suffer the little children ...' found so frequently in our catechisms. Gaelic type is used.

The prayers are the same as those in the English version except that the little verses *To the Infant Jesus* are omitted. The Serving of Mass is left out also and the Benediction hymns. The editor reverts to the old O'Reilly with the *Liodáin Mhuire*, not given in the English text. In the catechism itself, some messing with the sub-titles of the English version, so characteristic of the O'Reilly

6 On the title-page, besides M. H. Gill agus a Mhac, Sráid Uachdarach Ui Chonaill, Pádruig O Briain, Clodhadóir, 46, Sráid Chuf, Luach Pighin (gan laghdughadh). The same *Nihil Obstat* as in the 1891 edition Eduardus Maguire and *Imprimatur*, Gulielmus, Archiep. Dublin. Mens. Octobr. 1890.

editorial tradition, is corrected here, though not entirely satisfactorily. The print used for the notes to the lessons, the *Mion-mhíniughadh*, is a trifle small, but the overall printing and presentation is not undistinguished by comparison with the Williams edition; the catechism went out with the material grace denied it for so long.

The Tuam catechism we have mentioned as a main source of the tradition might be classified with some truth as a Connaught O'Reilly. It certainly had a lot of pure O'Reilly blood. The prayer sequences, morning and evening, follow the O'Reilly tradition with little variation. In several instances too, throughout the text, O'Reilly's is the model, but generally speaking and quite often word for word Donlevy's catechism is the choice, so much so that the Tuam text is fairly described as a 'Short Donlevy'.

6

A Catechism from Paris

In comparison with the lowly beginnings of the catechism by Michael O'Reilly, 'the popish priest of Cavan', the origins of Donlevy's effort were really something. It saw the light in Paris, the first city of Europe. It came with the approbation of the King of France, the Archbishop of Tuam, the Bishops of Kildare and Killaloe and four Doctors of the Sorbonne, and in a decorative Irish type of considerable beauty, cut in Paris, which it shares with only one other book. It was patronized and doubtless paid for by 'a very worthy Gentleman, Philip-Joseph Perrot, Lord of the Mannor of Barmon, and other Territories, Knight of the Royal Order of S. Michael etc.' And the author, M. Andrew Donlevy, Licentiate of Laws and Prefect of the Irish Community at Paris, was himself a man of sufficient consequence in the city of his adoption to have gained the favourable notice of Louis XV's Cardinal Fleury.

The catechism was printed in 1742 by James Guerin, at S. Thomas of Aquin's in St James-street, with double title-page, Irish and English:

An Teagusg Críosduidhe, Do réir Ceasda agus Freagartha, air na tharruing go bunudhasach as Bréithir hSoilléir Dé, agus as Toibreachaibh fíorghlana oile.

The Catechism or Christian Doctrine, By Way of Question and Answer, Drawn chiefly from the express Word of God, and other pure Sources.

By way of preface there is a *Forfhógra* or *Advertisement*, of considerable length, Irish and English successively, from which we learn Donlevy's own view of the origin and sources of the work and its aims. The catechism is printed in the two languages, side by side, the Irish version to the left. Donlevy was a trifle concerned about his English, the work being 'translated, upon a second Thought, perhaps too literally, from the *Irish*'. He was none too sure about his Irish either and he knew James Guerin had his own problems.

An absence of upwards of 31 Years from one's native Country, and the

59

profound Ignorance of the Printer, who understood not one Word of either Language, will be sufficient Apology, for the Faults of both the Languages, and the Press.

He is anxious about more culpable errors which he discusses in a brief study at the end of the work on 'The Elements of the Irish Language'. These arise, as he saw them, in either language, from what he calls 'the Fancy of Writing as People speak'. Examples in Irish would be *sgan* for *agus gan*, *sgo* for *agus gur*, and in English, where he saw a more marked decline in standards and which he traces to the beginning of the reign of Charles the Second, he rattles off quite a list which judicious English writers, so he thinks, would look upon as 'a great *Abuse*'- I'll, you'll, he'll,won't, don't, t'other and so on. Yet, although strict about the proper use of the parts of speech and proud of his own tongue as a medium, 'a very Ancient *Mother-Language*, and one of the smoothest in *Europe*', his first concern is effective teaching of the faith. He claims to use the plainest and most obvious Irish, preferring as he says in the preface to follow the example of St Augustine who would 'rather to be censured by Grammarians than misunderstood of the People'.

He shared this concern for the need of the people with several of his predecessors in the field of continental Irish catechisms, notably O'Heoghusa and Theobald Stapleton. O'Heoghusa, of bardic stock, his family having been hereditary poets to the Maguires of Fermanagh, was sensitive about the reaction of his class to his under-ornate style and he explains his reasons for it. Stapleton had no association whatever with bards or their families, he was in fact of Engish extraction, but he dearly loved the language and urged it strongly as a medium of instruction. He was all for simplicity. He even anticipated An t-Athair Peadar by recommending that Irish should be written as it was spoken by ordinary people; he simplified the spelling and used Roman characters. Donlevy went a distance with all this, if he did draw the line when *cainnt na ndaoine* got a bit sloppy. He took care to be understood, frequently giving in a footnote the alternative form of a word used in the text though not 'in some Cantons of the Kingdom'. His Irish is certainly plain, reads easily once you become accustomed to the unusual type-face (assuming of course that you grew up with the gaelic script), and the use of abbreviations is minimal compared, say, to John Dowley's *Suim Bhunadhasach*. But the catechism style that really appealed to Donlevy, the one he tried to reproduce, though with no great success was Antony Gearnon's.[1] Gearnon had little use for tiresome discussions on

60

the state of the language, he was in no way self-conscious about his performance, he just wrote with his mind on the people he wanted to instruct and to form in piety. His *Parrthas an Anma*, (*The Paradise of the Soul*), was Donlevy's pick of the large catechisms published in the previous century.

Donlevy had another practical concern. He felt he had to sell the idea of a bulky catechism to people used only to the little abridgments. He is quick to point out that they are concerned with only half the work in their hands, since it comes in two languages. The catechism in fact had something short of 900 formulas which is not unreasonably large considering that the *Scottish Catechism of Christian Doctrine* published at the end of the era, in 1954, had 700. Many of Donlevy's answers, however, were quite lengthy, in the style of the *Summa* of Canisius. Donlevy's work was of course aimed at the more advanced pupil and, primarily perhaps, though he does not say so, he had in mind the priest or other catechist who would use the work as a source book for instruction after the manner of the standard Roman Catechism in the hands of parish priests. He argues justly that advanced instruction was necessary, and he was doubtless right in his claim that the scarcity of the large Irish catechisms of the previous century was presenting a problem. He is no doubt right, too, in claiming that it is, as he puts it, 'a dangerous and pernicious and *vulgar* Mistake' to equate instruction with the repetition by heart, '*Children-like*' of a short catechism; though he does seem to underestimate the range of texts like O'Reilly's if competently explained.

For all that he is shrewdly conscious of the value of abridgments. He promises his readers in the first page of the preface that towards the end they will come upon an abridgment in Irish rhyme, 'composed upwards an Age ago by the zealous and learned F. Bonaventure O'Heoghusa of the Order of St Francis'. O'Heoghusa's *Suim Bhunadhasach an Teagaisg Chríosdaighe a nDán*, which accompanied his catechism, is that very medieval-style collection of memory tags on the creed, prayer, commandments, sacraments and the usual string of virtues and vices conveniently emphasised by number. Lined up here in the elegant Paris type, pp. 487f., they make a pretty picture at the end of Donlevy's long day.[2]

1 It is a curiosity of Donlevy's *Forfhógra* that it does not mention the texts on which the catechism leant so considerably. Perhaps he thought it enough to acknowledge the Louvain Franciscans and O'Hussey in particular.

2 There are seventeen verse forms in the *Suim*: An Chré. An Phaidior. An Beannchadh Muire. Deich nAitheanta De. Aiteanta na hEagluisi. Na Seacht Sacramainte. Na Trí Subháilce Diadha. Na Ceithre Subháilce Cairdionálta. Seacht

Rhyme is not given the role in Donlevy's text, nor for that matter in any of our Irish catechisms, that it has in O'Heoghusa's. The couplets on the Church precepts are incorporated in the Irish text, the ones we have met already in O'Reilly's and which turn up also in the Irish version of the original Butler catechism.[3] The rhyme of the Ten Commandments, however, the only other verse-form used in the catechism proper, is not O'Heoghusa's but O'Reilly's and the form consistently repeated by the Butler catechisms in Irish.[4] In view of this fondness in our traditions for versifying the decalogue, O'Heoghusa's couplets must have a special interest. We can of course only reproduce in Roman script:

> Ná hAdhair bréig Dhia ná iodhal,
> ná mionnaigh Ainm Dé gan chúis.
> Domhnach lá an Tighearna Críosd
> Coimhéid do shíor é go búidh.

> Onóraigh hAithre gan ghruig.
> Ná déin Marbhadh, Drúis, ná goid.
> Ná déin breig-fhiaghnaisi air Neach.
> A mhaoin, ná a bhean ná hiarr dhuit.

Donlevy's 'pure Sources' for his work, other than the express Word of God, are the ancient Fathers, the decrees of Popes and Councils, the Roman Catechism, the works of Thomas Aquinas, Francis de Sales, Charles Borromeo, Cardinal Bellarmine and the Roman Missal and Ritual. The references are carefully tagged, like Scripture texts, chapter and verse. They appear on the margin of the preface and throughout the text, in italics, at the end of an answer. Canisius did the same thing on the margin of his *Summa*, entering some 1100 Scripture quotations and more than

dTiodhlaicthe an Spioraid Naoimh. Seacht nOibre Corpordha na Trócuire. Seacht nOibre Spioradálta na Trócuire. Na hOcht nDronga Beannaighthe. Na Seacht gCeinn-Pheacaidhe Marbhtha. Ceathra Pheachadh bhíos ag Sgréachadh air Dhia ag iarradh díoghaltais. Sé Pheachadh an aghuidh an Spioraid Naoimh. Na Cúig Céadfadh Corpordha. Na Ceathra Críocha Déighionacha.

3 There are two Irish versions of Archbishop Butler's own text, *Suim Athghar an Teagasg Criosduighe*, Dublin 8vo, 78 pp., 'Printed by J. Boyce, Bookseller, No 29, Merchant's-quay near Bridge-street, and sold by Miss Everard, Navan', copy 1784 printing British Museum, and *An Teagusg Creesdeegh*, 'Chun Aós óg no Leanavh do Heugusg', Cork, Thomás do Wheete and Shéumus O'Haly, 8vo. pp. 56, 1792, copy in the National Library. The verse form is in the Boyce printing.

4 Including the Peadar Ua Laoghaire text. This catechism, dating from the time of William Coppinger who was bishop of Cloyne and Ross from 1791, the year of Butler's death, until 1830, is clearly a short version of Butler's own text. The English version was attributed to Coppinger in the early printings.

400 from the Fathers, a performance that prompted the German Bishop Knecht to comment: 'It is not the genius of a particular man that speaks to us here: it is the spirit and the voice of the Church'. Knecht's observation was not original. O'Heoghusa had the same to say about his work, expressed in the last stanza of the poem with which he introduces his catechism to the reader: the work not deserving commendation because it is his but because it is the undiluted teaching of God. Donlevy, in his turn, presumes a similar elevation of his efforts as a reward for his orthodoxy:

As the Method or Order of the Work, is the same with that of the *Catechism of the Council of Trent*, and the Matter thereof is chiefly taken out of the *sacred Scripture*, the Writings of the *holy Fathers*, and Decisions of the *Church*, it ought not to be considered the Work of a miserable Man, but of *God himself*, and his *chosen Servants*.

The miserable man, nonetheless, while laying no claim to genius, did regard his catechism as a sort of *summa* and was none too modest in estimating its rank. He had written, he thought, an Irish Catechism 'wherein the Commandments, Sacraments, Prayers, &c. are treated more at Large than in any *Irish*, or perhaps, *English Catechism*, that hitherto appeared in Print.'

This careful acknowledgment of orthodox sources without bothering about what one might call copyright material is very Tridentine. O'Heoghusa and Stapleton, for example, leant heavily on Bellarmine's teacher's book, *Copiosa Explanatio Doctrinae Christianae*, translating whole passages, word for word, without reference to source. Indeed phrases, sentences and longer scripts occur so frequently in different texts that it becomes quite a piece of research to discover who first made it up. An instance in point is Donlevy's handling of the worship of saints, their images and relics, which was an issue throughout the era. It seems clear he was familiar with the appropriate passages in Turberville's *Doway* catechism, and the same may be said of the *Doway's* dependence on the sixth chapter of Bellarmine's explanatory text.

Donlevy's heaviest textual dependence was, of course, on O'Reilly's catechism. We have already been supplied with the arithmetic of similarity between the formulas of the two catechisms. Donlevy's effort is always a variation by way of elaborating on the same theme. Both texts begin with a formula that sets the catechism in this tradition:

O'R: Q. Who created you, and made you in the world?
A. God.

D: Q. Who created and placed you in the World?
A. Almighty God. *Gen* 1.27. *Eph.* 3.9

One must judge for oneself the relative quality of the performances. I have always been moved by O'Reilly's pithy but sensitive adjudgment of one aspect of the husband-wife relationship:

O'R: Q. How must a husband behave towards his wife?
A. He must use her lovingly, carefully and tenderly, like a part of his own body, as Christ doth his spouse, the Church.

D: Q. How is the Husband to behave himself in Regard to his Wife?
A. As Christ behaves himself in Regard of the Church, that is, lovingly and carefully; for the Wife is a Member of the Husband, as we are all Members of Christ. *Gen.* 2.23, 24. *S. Mar.* 10, 8. *Ephes.* 5. 25, 28, 30, 31.

Donlevy's work is not confined to this sort of elaboration of O'Reilly's formulas. He develops the themes, treating the matter, to use his own phrase 'at Large'. His doctrinal and moral themes are presented defensively in the counter-Reformation tradition. The true Church is 'the holy Catholick Roman Church, whose visible Head is the Pope'. This being so, it is but just that true children of the Church should give great thanks to God for making them children of so great and so good a Mother. 'Hereticks' are named. Do they sin against the First Commandment? 'They do for certain; because they do not sincerely believe what the Roman Catholick Church holds. All those likewise do sin, who either by Word or Deed shew an Inclination or Bent to Heresy, by hearing their Prayers, or Instructions, or otherwise.' *S. Mat.* 18, 17. *Rom.* 10.10.

Some contemporary writers, adapting to our vastly different circumstances, and bemoaning the lack of ecumenism in the era of dark struggle, detect a dimension of controversialism in the 18th century catechisms that was happily absent in those of the previous century. The truth seems to me a matter of emphasis in relation to the function of the catechism in building up the spiritual life or in defending the faith against virulent attack. Our Irish language catechisms of the 17th century, from O'Heoghusa's on, were addressed to the Irish in exile but in a protected and religiously privileged condition. They had a heavily spiritual, even ascetic slant. The later catechisms, from the time of O'Molloy's *Lucerna Fidelium*, published in 1676, were looking towards the people at home, in a condition of siege and in need of defensive weaponry. In point of fact when the earlier Irish catechisms did touch on the controverted issues they could be very blunt. Gearnon's *Parrthas an Anma*, beloved of Donlevy, was fiercely anti-Protestant in the appropriate section, denouncing heretics without quarter and naming Luther for his sins as the tainted source that barred

64

them from holiness.[5] Donlevy was forthright also, a heretic was a heretic; but he presented the case technically and argued at a personal level with restraint and with an effort at good sense and good will. This is particularly so in one sensitive area where the faith was under heavy pressure and Catholic ire easily aroused. Do not Catholics pray to, and serve images? Donlevy presses his case with courtesy and an appeal for fair play. I think the passage not untypical:

... as we have the Charity to believe upon their Word, that they neither pray to, nor adore either the Communion Table or the Bread and Wine, they receive kneeling; so should they, it seems, have the like Charity for us, seeing the whole Church assembled at Trent, even all of us, Men, Women and Children do openly declare and constantly profess, that we neither pray to, nor adore Images; that we certainly know, they can neither see, nor hear, nor help us ...

Where Donlevy was all one with the *Parrthas* was the way in which he mingled piety and devotion with instruction. He saw his work, as Gearnon did his, as 'interspersed with short *Forms* of acts of Devotion, and Prayers, to be used on different Occasions, and particularly before and after Confession and Communion, Morning and Evening, and at other Times; so, that it may serve as a Sort of *Prayer-book* ...'. In this respect both were in the tradition of St Peter Canisius, at least in some of the German editions of his smaller catechisms. In line of course with O'Reilly also except that O'Reilly, as we have seen, assembled his devotions together at the beginning of the little work, his abridgment was so slight.

Donlevy, moreover, employed a device that is so modern, the introduction of a pious reflection at the end of a lesson by way of spiritual summary. This he called the *Fruit of this Lesson*. Unfortunately he employed it twice only, if I mistake not, in the first two lessons of the catechism proper. Perhaps he was running out of space. But his over-all plan survived. Prayers keep popping up in every appropriate place and the catechism ends with a lengthy lesson *Of Meditation or Mental Prayer*. Here again the intention outstripped the performance. Unlike Gearnon's *An Deachmadh Rann don Pharrathas-So*, which brings one through the sacred passion, step by step, Donlevy is content with a treatise on Mental Prayer, pressing its necessity for the spiritual life, indeed for salvation, and in a climate heavy with foreboding for those who neglect it. He does give some helpful advice on the ease and blessings of ejaculatory prayer and on the practice of union with God in the midst of one's daily preoccupations. But this is not

5 *Parrthas*, Ó Fachtna ed., pp. 54f.

quite the same thing, and when the question is raised of the method or order of our meditation he replies blandly:

Many good Prayer-books treat very amply of the Method of Meditation. Let them be consulted: This is no place to make a long Dissertation upon Mental Prayer.

Yet this is precisely what he was doing, and he had forgotten what he had been saying in the introductory passage from his *Advertisement*, quoted above, about the 'Sort of *Prayer-book*' he would like his work to be and for such precisely 'as have no better, nor much Time to spare'.

Donlevy advises *every one* 'to bestow about Half an Hour on this Prayer; and that in the Morning, as it is recommended to us in so many Passages of the *Holy Scripture*. Eccli. 39.6. Ps. 62.7. Ps. 118. 148'. This will appear a bit much. But he is not quite so exacting as his mentor, Gearnon. Donlevy has this formula of instruction for the good Christian going to bed, right out of the *Parrthas*:[6]

Q. What do you do, whilst you are taking off your Cloaths?

A. I beg of God, through the Stripping of Jesus Christ before he was *crucified*, to strip me entirely of the inordinate Desires of the World and the Flesh.

The *Parrthas* sends the good man to bed with the same pious disposition but resolved to rise at midnight for the *iarmheirghe* or matins. Gearnon urges this practice on the not unreasonable grounds that many Irish people did it. Nor was it so outlandish in a society not only modelled spiritually on the monastic ideal but so often grouped as well in large households. Gearnon was a gentleman and he clearly envisaged the Big House. Nor was Donlevy much different in outlook. He speaks in his treatise on meditation of Heads of a Family, of Servants and Workmen 'who are under Subjection', and implies the idea of morning assembly for prayer as not only practicable but as a religious duty, almost binding.

A word about the structure of Donlevy's text. He follows O'Reilly very closely. The end for which God placed us in the world is to know, love and serve him, and thereby merit life everlasting, as Paul points out to the Thessalonians in the epistle, 4:3. To answer the end we must do the four things, the *ceithre neithe*, to believe as the Creed tells us, to keep the commandments, receive the sacraments and practise prayer. In the ancient tradition

6 Compare the *Parrthas*, ed. cit., pp. 30f. with Donlevy's.

of Augustine, the Creed was seen as response to Faith, the commandments to Charity, prayer to the virtue of Hope, with the sacraments fitted in as neatly as one could. Like O'Reilly, Donlevy gets a bit lost as the plan unfolds. Faith, as the virtue, is defined as he opens up on the Creed, Hope introduces prayer, but Charity that urges and supports obedience to God's law is lost out in the appropriate place where it is so stressed in the prototypal Jesuit texts and in the *Parrthas*; it is given its say in the chapter on Christian Virtues. Which goes to show how dependent Donlevy was on O'Reilly's catechism.

He does depart from O'Reilly in some respects. Not of consequence. He inserts the virtues, beatitudes etc., those loose ends lined up in convenient files in the later medieval tradition, after the treatment of sin in his second part, where O'Reilly elects for the final section on Hope and Prayer. He has a full lesson too on the Holy Mass in his fourth part, the one omitted in the original O'Reilly texts, and he adds lessons on Holy Water and on 'The Beads', alternately named in both languages, 'The Crown of the Blessed Virgin', before closing with his chapter on Mental Prayer.

7

The Community Prefect

In the preface to the third edition of the catechism the Maynooth historian, Renehan, provides a tentative outline of Andrew Donlevy's origins and career. He is said to have been born and to have received his early education in or near the town of Ballymote. The town is quaintly located by Renehan 'in the county of Sligo, and diocese of Achonry, but on the confines of Elphin, and not far from the counties of Mayo and Roscommon.' The family had a foothold in Achonry and Elphin and continued to supply priests to both dioceses for another two generations, Donlevy's nephews and grand-nephews. They were folk who lived in comfortable circumstances, a typical Tridentine clerical family, the social background never less than respectable. Andrew's arrival in France is placed in 1710, which squares with his own statement that as he wrote the catechism he was some thirty-one years away from home. Renehan's other dates, however, do not fit in with the information supplied on Donlevy's tombstone. He was not born in 1694, nor was he alive in 1761.

On a visit to Paris in the early 1880's James O'Laverty, the historian of the diocese of Down and Connor, found the tombstone in the chapel of the old Irish College, the *Collège des Lombards*, in the Rue des Carmes.[1] He found it under the matting in front of the altar along with a number of other 'funereal slabs', all of them clearly legible and suggesting to him that he had not come upon the actual graves. The slabs were all the same size, about two and a half feet in length. The inscription on Donlevy's read as follows.

---

1 *I.E.R.*, January 1892 issue, pp. 86-89. There has been a little flurry of interest in the Irish College in Paris and its affairs aroused by the tricentenary of the College des Lombards, 1977. See *The Irish-French Connection 1578-1978*, edited by the Irish College Archivist, Fr Liam Swords, Irish College publication, 1978. Fr Swords tells me in a letter from the College, dated 2 February 1978, that the Chapel of the Lombards is still there, the Donlevy inscription surviving, although now barely legible. The chapel is still used for sacred worship also. A Mass in Irish was celebrated there in 1977, the year of the 'Tricentenaire', Bishop Daly of Ardagh and Clonmacnoise presiding.

Hic jacet
M. Andreas Donlevy
Communitatis Clericorum
Hibernorum per 24
Annos Praefectus et
Ejusdem Restaurator
Seu potius Fundator
Obiit die 7a Xbris anno
1746 Aetatis 66
Requiescat in Pace

The thirty-one years' absence from the homeland does not, therefore, relate to his departure as a lad for Paris to train for the priesthood in the Irish College. We have no reliable information about Donlevy's early years. What we do know of him is linked with the College, and there we must look for him, especially in the community of pre-ordination clerical students of which he was the effectual founder and which he served as prefect in difficult circumstances during the last twenty-four years of his life.[2]

There is abundant evidence of an effective and indeed forceful presence of Irish seminarians in the University of Paris from the earliest Tridentine time, but it was not until 1677, some three years before the birth of Donlevy, that the first Irish College proper was acquired, a delapidated 14th century institution known as the Lombard College. The two influential Irish ecclesiastics who managed to secure it, Doctors Maginn and Kelly, restored it at their own expense with generous French assistance. The Lombard was the original 'Community', and it became the centre for the Irish colony in Paris; it was here James II held court on his return to France after the Boyne, and it was here in the early 18th century during the difficult years of the reign of Queen Anne that several of the Irish hierarchy lived out their exile and died.

One French benefactor, the Abbé Bailly, initiated a development that was to have a vital bearing on the Donlevy story. Some time before his death in 1692 the Abbé provided a house in the Rue Traversine for Irish clerics studying in Paris, as distinct from priests. The house was duly occupied and the upshot was there were now two student bodies, the one for priests in the Lombard and the other for the younger unordained clerics in the nearby Rue Traversine. Donlevy was charged with the priestly formation of these young men, becoming Prefect of Clerics in 1722.[3] By this

2   The main source of my narrative is *The Irish College in Paris from 1578 to 1901*, Rev. Patrick Boyle, CM, Dublin, 1901.

3   Boyle, op. cit. p. 217, lists Donlevy as Superior of the Clerics, 1728-1746, the Rev. John O'Neill following 1746-1761. But the inscription on the Donlevy

69

time a considerable tension had developed between the priest-students and the younger aspirants in the course of which Donlevy's personality and influence were to prove major factors.

The clerics in the Rue Traversine were badly off and found themselves in debt in 1707. They appealed to the king for some share in the endowments of the Lombard College on the grounds that the letters patent of 1623, long before the Irish took possession, mentioned *ecoliers* or students as liable for benefit. The outcome of this appeal was the union of the two communities under the one roof, namely the Lombard, priests and students to follow the same rule and share the same facilities. This arrangement had, apparently, only relative success. There were squabbles, over money for one thing, the clerics being at the disadvantage of not having Mass intentions to support them, and by 1717 the University Rector intervened, insisting on a revision of the college rules. Such harmony as emerged from this initiative was shortlived too. By 1724 the clerics, now led by their Prefect, Donlevy, were again appealing to the king. This time the affair was referred to the Archbishop of Paris on whose advice, and indeed through Donlevy's influence with Cardinal Fleury, a substantially new code of rules was drawn up for the government of the College and ratified by the royal authority in 1728.

The royal *Arret* is a formidable document consisting of a preamble and twenty-eight articles.[4] It acknowledges the existence of the two communities, 'une des Pretres étudiants, e l'autre des Clercs aussy étudiants'. The most detailed provisions are made to ensure that both parties would equally enjoy the benefits of the College. There was to be an equal number of priests and clerical students and — to meet a root cause of the Irish squabbles — the places were to be shared equally by the four Irish ecclesiastical provinces. Donlevy's influence secured a firm position for the unordained: the juniors were henceforth to enjoy their full share of all the financial endowments of the College, they were to have their own quarters, carefully specified in Article 16, and their own refectory. They were thus established as a viable community within the Lombard and so remained until about 1769 when they transferred to a college of their own in the Rue du Cheval Vert, later to be known as the Rue des Irlandais. This of course was after Donlevy's time, but he can be truly said to have been the founder of the Irish College in terms of the 'Communitas Clericorum Hibernorum', the College of modern times and the

tomb, printed also by Boyle, p. 227, gives him twenty-four years in office. I am following the inscription.
4 Printed in full by Boyle, pp. 182-196.

Alma Mater of the 'Community Boys' as the Irish priests it nurtured came to be known in the homeland.[5]

The second object of the 1728 *Arret* was to secure harmony in the internal government of the College. There was nothing especially new in placing the College under the control of the University authorities and the Archbishop of Paris. The Rector of the University had the right of visitation and the College was bound by the University's general rules and academic discipline. The ultimate control by the Paris ecclesiastical authorities, moreover, went back to the time of the original Lombard College. What was new was the Archbishop's insistence on direct personal intervention: Article 1 specified that the Irish Community was subject to the Archbishop and his nominees. The government of the College was to consist of four Provisors and the Prefect of Clerics. The Provisors, one from each province, would be duly elected by the students of philosophy and theology and confirmed by the Archbishop who would then allot them their duties, the one as Principal, the others as Prefect of the Priest-Students, Sacristan (responsible for liturgical training) and Bursar. The Prefect of the Clerics was an appointment reserved absolutely to the Archbishop, an arrangement, one might suspect, inspired by Donlevy. According to Article 17 the Prefect was to be responsible for the spiritual and temporal welfare of the juniors, he was to preside over their studies and to form them in piety.

The student involvement in the administration of the College must occur to us as anticipating later and more liberal days. Students were given a direct say in the choice of their superiors, albeit a limited one in that their candidate had to be a native of the province for which they were voting and one who held a degree not less than that of Master of Arts in the University of Paris. They were further given the right of representation at the quarterly and annual rendering of accounts by the Bursar and Prefect of Clerics, the equitable distribution of the monies being an especially sensitive issue: one ventures again to suspect the hand of Donlevy who may well have felt the need of support. But the student involvement was in fact no great break with Tridentine tradition: it was rather directed towards easing the tensions and eliminating the squabbles that plagued the College. The rules of conduct outlined in the *Arret* were very rigid, much in line with the exaltation of authority that marked the seminary regime everywhere prior to Vatican II. The priest students no less than the clerics were regimented and restrained, always under supervision. The list of severely punishable offences detailed in Article 26 must

5 Boyle, p. 41.

sound familiar to erstwhile Tridentine seminarians, given the opportunities for villainy the *Arret* envisaged. Those who were convicted of having frequented a *cabaret de vin, de biere ou de café*, who slept outside the College without permission, became inebriated within or without the walls, gave way to violence or the like, were to be *chassés du Collége sans espérance d'y rentrer*. Lesser offences such as being found in somebody else's room, rated in Maynooth terminology as a 'grave irregularity', was punishable at the discretion of the Principal.

On the issue of the *Arret*, in addition to the traditional Major-Superiors, the Chancellor of Notre Dame and the Abbot of St Victor's, the Archbishop nominated as his special representative the Abbé de Vaubrun who was a professor in the Sorbonne. It proved a happy appointment. The Abbé helped in the extension of the College buildings and more especially in the reconstruction of the chapel which was carried out by a notable architect named Boscry. It was in this chapel, a hundred and fifty years later, that Fr James O'Laverty found the funeral slab under the matting, and it was here or in the environs that Donlevy was laid to rest. De Vaubrun died in 1746, bequeathing a sum of 30,000 livres to the Irish College. Donlevy was spared the worry of how much this windfall might benefit his clerics: he died just before the Abbé.

Unfortunately the royal decree, for all its care and apparent wisdom, did not solve the Irish question in Paris. The final article of the *Arret* had set aside all contenders for the office of Provisor and 'pour cette fois seulement' appointed the four who were to hold office until 1730 when the elections on the lines decided would take place. When the elections did eventually take place, in 1731, the men appointed by the king were voted back to office. But when the next election came up in 1734 new Provisors were chosen, and this led to such further trouble that in 1737 the Archbishop reverted to direct rule and began making the appointments himself, as he did in respect of the Prefect of Clerics in accordance with the *Arret*.

The main cause of the fresh tension seems to have sprung from an idea gaining ground that the Irish Church would be better served by discontinuing the practice of sending priests to the Lombard at all. Donlevy was a strong supporter of this movement, if not indeed its originator. The priest-students, ordained at home and without formal ecclesiastical training, were the products of a system that encountered very serious difficulties but on the whole seemed to have been working reasonably well. Naturally they were up in arms when their position was challenged. They appealed to the Irish bishops who by and large supported them. The point made

72

by the priests and their bishops was that it was they, the priest *étudiants* of the Lombard, who mainly supported the Irish Mission. The priests came to Paris ordained for their respective dioceses and while, no doubt, some of them, tempted by the flesh-pots of Europe, never returned (the 1728 *Arret* provided regulations to ensure that they would return), they came back on the whole and were the backbone of the Irish priesthood. The priests asserted in their defence that between 1694 and 1734, a period of forty years, the community of clerics gave no more than twenty-five priests to the homeland. They alleged that many clerical students lost their vocations in France, attracted by the opportunities open to them in the army and the professions, or forgot the Irish Mission on ordination and did well for themselves by staying put.

Donlevy, being the students' man, was bound to draw the ire of such bishops as backed the priests. He was readily accused of using his office to bolster the case for the unordained only. 'Permit me to repeat to you', wrote the Bishop of Raphoe in 1735, 'that I know only two missioners from your community in this whole province; and if the project of giving over the College to the juniors succeeds, it will be all over with the mission here, for thereby we lose our only supply'.[6] Donlevy was not, however, the only enemy. In 1737 Dr McDonogh, the Bishop of Kilmore who figured in our O'Reilly story, was the leader of a group of bishops who petitioned Corsini, the Cardinal Protector of the Irish Church, to remove Bourk and Daton as well as Donlevy from their posts in the College on the grounds that in refusing to accept ordained priests they 'were doing more harm to the Irish Mission than all the magistrates of Ireland'.[7] John Bourk and Walter Daton had been among those appointed Provisors by the king and confirmed in office by the election of 1731. They were dropped in the controversial election of 1734 but apparently found their way back through the squabbles that ensued. In the event the affair was patched up after the usual representations and investigations and the *status quo* was maintained with more or less harmony until 1769 when the matter was resolved by the establishment of the College for clerical students in the future Rue des Irlandais. The priests remained at the Lombard College until the Revolution, while the *Communitas Clericorum Hibernorum* continued to supply the Irish Church until the outbreak of the Second World War in 1939.

6 Boyle, p. 36.
7 See Hugh Fenning, 'Michael MacDonogh OP, Bishop of Kilmore, 1728-46', *I.E.R.*, September 1966, p. 143. The argument of these bishops was that those ordained after studies in Paris were good for nothing when they returned home but teaching French.

Despite these internal problems and the image of constant squabbling among themselves the Irish were stubbornly orthodox and undivided in the controversies affecting Catholic doctrine and discipline. They stood by the Pope and by those champions of the papacy, the anti-Gallican Jesuits. Precisely because the Jesuits were so unpopular in Paris they invited one of them to preach in their College chapel on St Patrick's Day 1730. They did it very pointedly, selecting Tournemine, a personality who was bound to arouse the antagonism of the authorities,[8] which is just what happened, for the invitation was promptly quashed by the University Rector. A few years later,when the trouble involving Donlevy was at its height, there was found to be no support worthwhile among the Irish in Paris for the Jansenist proclivities of the time. The papal nuncio, Monsignor Dolci, had inquired about the orthodoxy of the Irish and came up with this glowing tribute on 9 July 1736:

In the Irish College, consisting of about one hundred persons, profession is made of the most sound doctrine, nor is anyone tolerated therein who is in the least suspected. Moreover, amongst about two hundred Irish priests who are in this city and diocese, there are hardly two or three who have appealed, and they are held in execration by all others of their nation.[9]

The Irish were reacting in the tradition of their student forbears. It was the Irish students in Paris of the previous century who launched a counter-attack against the emerging Jansenist heresy that helped substantially towards the condemnation of the famous Five Propositions by the papal Bull *Cum Occasione* of 31 May 1653. It would be pointless to attempt to assess the French influence on our catechesis without cognisance of the Jansenist issue. The heresy owes its name to the Netherlands Bishop of Ypres Cornelis Jansen, whose book *Augustinus* contained the objectionable theology. His teaching was certainly startling. It claimed, and on the authority of St Augustine, that our Lord did not die for all men, that such as were offered divine grace could not resist it and that there were those, just men, who despite their good will and

8 I take him to be the Joseph René de Tournemine who had been an intimate of Montesquieu until they quarrelled. Rousseau mentions the break in the *Confessions* with a note of admiration for Montesquieu who told everybody after the rupture: 'Listen to neither Father Tournemine nor to myself when we speak of each other, for we are no longer friends'.

9 Quoted in Boyle, p. 39. But for a rather less flattering if cautious assessment of Jansenist influence in the Ireland of the previous century, see Donal F. Cregan, 'The Social and Cultural Background of a Counter-Reformation Episcopate 1618-1660' in *Studies in Irish History presented to R. Dudley Edwards*, 1980, pp. 110f.

their best efforts could not keep some of the commandments for want of sufficient grace. The influence of Jansen might have proved negligible were it not for the activities of his adherents in France. It was there, in Paris, that the principles of the *Augustinus* were reduced to practice in a book by Antoine Arnauld that is said to have made the fortune of Jansenism, *De la Fréquente Communion*.[10] The conditions for frequent communion as set out in Arnauld's work were so strict and rigid as entirely to belie its title: only those who had attained the pure love of God might receive regularly, nor might any who had committed mortal sin approach the rails at all for some months at least, during which time they would have done the penance prescribed, awaiting absolution until it was complete.

It was the success of the book among the faithful at large more than the movement's progress in religious institutes such as the famous convent of Port Royal, controlled by Arnauld's sisters, that prompted a vigorous orthodox reaction.[11] St Vincent de Paul was quick to notice the marked decrease in the numbers receiving Holy Communion. When battle was joined blow followed blow, papal denunciations of the new doctrine accepted and rejected, the official Church and the King supporting authority, a small determined coterie of bishops, theologians in plenty — and the students — caught up in the fervour and excitement of change. In the midst of this turmoil, aided and abetted by 'Monsieur Vincent', the Irish priests in Paris made their move.

In February 1651 they drew up in Latin a declaration denouncing the propositions attributed to the Bishop of Ypres and supporting the Popes in their recurring condemnations. The document, published in defiance of an interdict imposed by the Rector of the University, had twenty-seven signatories, all priests.[12] It spoke about the damage being done by those who taught the new

10 See J. B. Dalgairns, *The Holy Communion*, Dublin, 1892, pp. 293f.

11 It was not simply that Arnauld had a wonderful way with him in writing on theolgocial subjects but that he had a keenly interested public. See Jean Delumeau, *Catholicism between Luther and Voltaire*, tr. Jeremy Moiser, London, 1977. Delumeau reveals that about the time Arnauld's book was published 49% of books printed in Paris were on religious themes: liturgical texts, theological treatises, mystical meditations, lives of the saints, stories of miracles. The biggest single category of hawked literature, about a quarter of the whole, was made up of books on devotions and indulgences, catechisms and carols. Delumeau is very good on Jansenism: opposed to affective devotions, against ostentation, anxious for a simplified liturgy, a combination of rigorism, Gallicanism, presbyterianism and distrust of absolute power.

12 Document reproduced by Boyle, pp. 22-24.

doctrines, preached, printed and spread them by word of mouth and, worst of all, in catechisms for simple folk. It spoke of their personal involvement as Irishmen, fearing lest the pernicious errors would penetrate to their own country — *patria nostra, Hibernia* — already for more than a hundred years plagued by the insults and vehement persecutions of heretics.

This was frank, and the reaction was extremely bitter.[13] Those of the signatories who were graduates of the University were summoned before the Rector, accused of subversion not only in acting in defiance of the Rector but against the laws of the realm and the liberties of the Gallican Church. They were condemned by a tribunal drawn apparently from the Faculty of Arts only. On appealing to the Faculty of Theology they were backed by the great majority of votes but, although this got them off the official hook, it did not save them from public opprobrium; they became the butt of lampoons playing on their impudence and their poverty. At least they were supported by an emotional commitment as deep as any sustaining the French of either side; news of Cromwell's doings in the homeland would have been coming through and the Irish priests must have taken a poor view of a Catholic Puritanism.

Cum Occasione was no more conclusive in the Jansenist affair than *Humanae Vitae* has proved to be in our contraception debate. There was a lull of sorts as the 17th century progressed, if only because people had got thoroughly sick of the monotonous rancour; but before the century was out an Oratorian priest, Paschase Quesnel, gave the heresy a new lease of life with a book of moral reflections on the New Testament that hit Paris with something of the force of *La Fréquente*. It repeated the doctrine which questioned God's universal will that all men should be saved, and it defended the irresistible power of divine grace in the souls of such as were offered it. Indeed Quesnel's book was so riddled with propositions at variance with traditional teaching that the papal Bull *Unigenitus* which condemned it in 1713 identified one hundred and one of them. The Bull was given a rough passage in France, especially in Paris where the vascillating archbishop, Cardinal Noailles, was little help to papal authority. In the resulting confusion, bedevilled by Gallican politics, the Jansenist ploy was an appeal to a general council against the Bull. Whereupon, Clement XI replied with another Bull that not only rejected the appeal but excommunicated the appellants. It was these 'appellants' Monsignor Dolci had in mind when he spoke of two or three of the Irish clergy in Paris who were held in execration by all others

13 For a detailed account of the affair see Thomas Wall 'Irish Enterprise in the University of Paris 1651-1653' in *I.E.R.*, August and September 1944.

of their nation.

At the time, then, that Donlevy was writing his catechism the challenge to orthodoxy uppermost in the French mind was Jansenism. There is, however, no overt reference to the French dissensions either in the approbations that accompany the catechism nor in Donlevy's own preface. Three Irish bishops, writing in Paris, warmly approved the catechism, their testimonies clearly showing that, whatever they may have thought of the quality of Donlevy's performance, they regarded his teaching as absolutely safe. Archbishop Michael O Gara of Tuam praised the book for its purity of Christian morality. The Bishop of Kildare, James Gallagher, the one who a few years previously as Bishop of Raphoe thought less well of Donlevy's activities, acknowledged that its sources were unquestionable and its sentiments Catholic. Bishop Patrick MacDonogh of Killaloe found it orthodox, with sound and pious doctrine and morals. Similar approval is expressed by theologians and colleagues. The Principal of the College, Francis Devereux, and two of its Provisors, Matthew MacKenna and Patrick Corr (whose tombstone was found under that matting alongside Donlevy's), agreed that 'the Sentiments are Catholick, the Devotion which it inspires is solid, and the Morality is exact, pious and profitable'. A fourth member of the staff, one Richard Hennessy, identified as Licentiate of the Sorbonne, subscribed his name to this solemn commendation.

Donlevy himself declares on the title page that the catechism is 'drawn from the express Word of God and other pure Sources' and he identifies these sources, as we have seen, with considerable care. The roots and aim of the catechism are clear: an early Jesuit-style text designed, in its defensive role, to protect Irish youth in their own country from an ascendant Protestantism. The Jansenist propositions are identified nonetheless (though not as such), the lesson *Of the Grace of God*, clearly written in the climate of the prevailing pressure. Donlevy declares emphatically that Christ died for all men, that it is for certain in our power with the help of divine grace to keep the commandments, that God does give sufficient grace to keep them, and that it is alas! most certain we can resist the grace he gives us, our capacity to co-operate or reject being the measure of our free will.

The evidence, therefore, points to the fact that doctrinal Jansenism, if it did come to this country at all, was not the product of the Irish College in Paris nor of the catechetical tradition we are examining. But the question remains of Jansenism as a temper of mind. It has been widely accepted and with considerable truth that the Tridentine message in Ireland down to our own time did

77

have a Jansenistic taint. Canon Sheehan's portrait of an Irish ecclesiastic in *The Blindness of Dr Grey* describes a sort of pastor who was not altogether uncommon well into this century. Those of us who are now elderly knew the last of them, admittedly not many, but we did meet them, men whose leanings would not be difficult to assess had they lived in the Paris of Arnauld or Quesnel. Time and again we heard them described so vividly by older priests, with ample illustrations of their quirks. I once heard a gentle saintly old missioner recounting at a dinner table with some lingering bitterness his boyhood experience of this Jansenist ambience.

The real harm done the faith by Jansenism was not in the heresy itself, for it pushed only a limited number into schism. The harm was in the way its adherents survived within the fold with mental reservations in respect of the Church's official teaching and their unyielding rigorism in the treatment of souls. As the years went by the heresy was recognised by everybody for what it was but its inflexible spirit continued to be widespread in the Church, especially in the teaching of moral theology and the practice of the sacraments. It is significant that in the area of conditions for reception of the Eucharist, the real testing ground for the influence of the heresy, the plain teaching of Trent that the Blessed Sacrament cancels our lesser sins and is the antidote for preserving us from serious ones was reluctantly accepted by the faithful before the reform of Pius X. Admittedly the hesitation in respect of frequent communion was not entirely due to Jansenist thought. The Church herself was hesitant about how far to go after a long tradition of infrequent reception following on the practice of daily communion in the early centuries. What Jansenism succeeded in doing was calling a halt to any growth in the Church's practice in accordance with the principles of Trent. Donlevy and his contemporaries in the Irish College were pressed from two sides, by the Protestants in the homeland and by the Jansenist fifth column on their door-step in Paris. Donlevy complained bitterly in his preface, he thought it very uncharitable, very unfair, that the orthodox faith should be accused on the one hand of moral laxity to the point of conniving at sin and on the other of spiritual severity by encroaching with anathemas on Gospel liberty. The pressure was heavy; perhaps it was too much. At any rate Donlevy's reaction tends to overemphasise Trent's penal legislation to the detriment of the divine mercy that is woven with such skill and beauty through all the pages of the Roman Catechism. Perhaps the comparison is not quite fair. Donlevy's is a question and answer text; Trent's is expository, with greater scope for those nuances in the development of a theme that secure a balance between justice and mercy.

Certainly Donlevy approaches his task with fierce zeal. He turns on 'vicious Catholics' with a pious indignation quite vicious in itself. His picture of the greater part of youth hurrying to destruction is intensely gloomy:

Young People, whereof more die before the Age of twenty, than all mankind after, are often deeply engaged, since first the in-bred Corruption of Nature began to spring out, in many secret Sins of Malice, Envy, Impurity, Revenge, Vanity, Sloth, &c. and remain therein, for Want of seasonable Instruction and Care, until an untimely Death snatches them away, in Punishment of their Transgressions . . . .[14]

Yet the Community Prefect cannot have been altogether unsuccessful in the delicate business of balancing law with love, for his boys and their successors in title bred in the same tradition by French emigré clergy in the infant Maynooth are the ones who laid the foundations of our Tridentine establishment. It was their tradition that made the people as we knew them before the change, strong in faith and full of a human gaiety and friendliness that proved so good for the tourist trade in the earlier unspoiled days of our affluence. Circumstances alter cases, of course, and our case was altered in half a generation out of all comparison with the experience of centuries before; yet it is a strange thing that when our young were living in the shadow of the cloister and subject to so much of Donlevy's 'seasonable instruction and care' they were a problem to nobody, least of all to themselves.

14 Advertisement to the Catechism, p. xxxv, and indeed *passim*. One is tempted to recall the judgment of Ronald Knox on Jansenism: 'Of all the Jansenist tricks none is more clearly un-Catholic than the readiness with which they assume their neighbour's damnation'; and on Jansenists: 'There is no *epikeia* (as the theologians call it) among these people, no margin of clemency': *Enthusiasm*, Oxford, 1950, pp. 203, 213.

8

The Donlevy texts

The catechism was published in Paris, as we have said, in 1742. It was printed bilingually, page to page, the Irish version in an elaborate and very rare Gaelic script. E. W. Lynam in *The Irish Character in Print 1571-1923* records the history of the Irish type.[1] It has been used, as far as is known, only once before, in 1732, in the *English-Irish Dictionary* of James Guerin. The type was to turn up some years after the catechism as an alphabet in Pierre Simon Fournier's *Manuel typographique* (1764-66). Then it disappeared. The type's fount, the only one in existence, was in the possession of Fournier at the time he was preparing his work, and Lynam suggests that Fournier's father may have been the one who cut it. The William Williams edition of O'Reilly's catechism also figures prominently in Lynam's study. This text was printed in a new Dublin Gaelic script, described by Lynam as 'the origin of our modern types'. Nor are these types the only links with the O'Reilly/Donlevy tradition. The Irish type O'Reilly might have used, if such a luxury were available to him, was Moxon's, cut in London at the end of the 17th century. Moxon's was the only Gaelic printed character on offer in these islands during O'Reilly's time and for more than half a century after his death. It was the one employed by earnest catechizers in the opposite camp such as John Richardson, the Rector of Annagh, who has helped us so considerably with the origins of the O'Reilly text.

Lynam's impatience with the near-exclusive use of Irish types in religious instruction filters through his scholarship. Speaking of the two books printed in the Paris type, the extent of his irritation is betrayed in a comment that in respect of the dictionary must apear singularly odd. 'It was a sign of happier days to come', he says, 'that these books were on the whole less concerned with religious propaganda than with the Irish language'. The catechism, it is true, did turn out to be of more lasting interest to linguists and typographers then to catechists, but this was quite accidental. So far from thinking 'the poor *Irish* Youth' had more than their

1 First published in 1924, reprinted by the Irish University Press, Shannon, with an Introduction by Alf MacLochlainn, in 1969: *passim* and especially pp. 14-19, 34-36.

fill of instruction in the faith, Donlevy felt they had much less than enough; that is why he wrote, and so he carefully explains.[2]

He was indeed an ardent Irish revivalist, indignant that the language should have been allowed to suffer so many alterations and corruptions so as to be on the brink of decay, 'as it really is', he argues heatedly, 'to the great dishonour and Shame of the *Natives*, who shall always pass every where for *Irish-Men*'. He was ahead of his times in calling for attention to the old valuable Irish manuscripts in public and private hands, 'those venerable Monuments of Antiquity', while doubtless insensitive to the predicament of the homeland in his rough denunciation of native neglect.[3] But all this was an aside. His real purpose was the teaching of the faith, and his problem was the problem of the catechists, his own students, who would have so many children speaking Irish only. The students might have too much French but they would certainly have too little Irish, and to meet this situation he added the little Irish grammar to the catechism, 'in favour of such', he says in the Preface, 'as would fain learn to read it; and thereby be useful to their neighbour'. Although James Guerin's printing is a bulky book, well bound in cardboard covers surfaced with light leather, the number of copies surviving from the first edition does not seem to be considerable. I have found copies in the National Library, the Franciscan Library at Killiney, the libraries of University College Cork, St Patrick's College, Thurles, and Mary Immaculate College of Education, Limerick. I am sure there are several others and there must be some few copies in private hands, I have one myself. In the latter half of the 18th century, however, there were enough of the catechisms about to keep the work alive, and the subsequent printings and editions would have flattered Donlevy.[4]

It was taken up considerably in England with several London reprintings of the English version. The oldest I have traced, in the National Library, is dated 1791, the preface somewhat abridged, well bound in leather for the modest sum of three and sixpence. A Scottish Jesuit, Alexander Clinton, was responsible

2　In the Advertisement *passim*, especially p. xxxviii, not to mention the catechism text.

3　See the section on the elements of the Irish language, pp. 506-7.

4　Since this was written, a good number of the Renehan texts in mint condition, together with a small number of somewhat damaged first editions, have been found during a clearing-out operation at Maynooth College. An t-Athair Pádraig Ó Fiannachta, the professor of Nua Ghaeilge at the college, has been making copies available to scholars on generous terms.

for another reproduction which, according to the bibliographer, Thomas Wall, was re-printed frequently for English readers. Wall has a piquant anecdote about this Clinton: 'He was an intimate friend of Challoner and was chaplain at Lulworth Castle until its proprietor, Thomas Weld, informed him in 1795 that 'he wished to continue friends, which could only be by his (Clinton's) leaving'.[5] Clinton left, coming to Ireland subsequently, where he died in 1800 at the age of seventy. His printing, published by J. P. Coghlan of London in 1796, I take to be the first of this edition. There was another re-print of the English text by the publisher, C. Dolman, of London, much later, in 1843. There are copies of the Coghlan and Dolman issues in the British Museum.

This printing record argues the popularity of the catechism in English, but there were critics. One of these, an Irish aristocratic priest, the Honourable and Reverend Jenico Preston, in a letter to Archbishop Troy took a poor view of Donlevy's treatment of usury and thought the catechism on the whole 'a very flimsy production', which no doubt it was if measured by the standards of a *summa* like that of Canisius. But Preston's statement in the same letter that 'the generality of catechisms used in Ireland are better than those used in England' seems odd in view of the fact that, apart from Donlevy's and William Gahan's *Exposition of the Small Catechism*, the advanced catechisms used by us at the time were in fact imported from England albeit frequently printed in Ireland — the works of Turberville, Challoner, Hay, Mannock etc.[6] It may have been that these latter were doing better in Ireland than in England where Donlevy was having such a good run.

The London printings of the English text are not rated as 'editions' since they cover only half the work. Two editions proper were published, both in Ireland, the Second Edition by the Rev. John McEncroe in 1822 and the Third in 1848 by our friend Dr Laurence F. Renehan, without the editor's name but with a preface that throws some light on our Gaelic catechetical history. We are told of Maynooth's special interest in publications in Irish. In the same year as McEncroe's edition of the catechism An t-Athair Domhnall Ó Súilliobháin brought out his translation of the

5 See 'Challoner's Contemporaries in Ireland', in *I.E.R.*, November 1946.

6 Preston was the son of Viscount Gormanston. He was in a position of influence and took an active part in Irish ecclesiastical politics. See his correspondence with Bishop Plunket of Meath in the third volume of Cogan's history of that diocese. I am indebted to Dr Patrick Wallace's work, already cited, for the quotes from the letter to Troy, Troy corrrespondence 1799 in the Dublin Diocesan Archives.

THE CATECHISM,

OR,

CHRISTIAN DOCTRINE,

BY WAY OF

QUESTION AND ANSWER,

DRAWN CHIEFLY FROM

THE EXPRESS WORD OF GOD,

AND

OTHER PURE SOURCES.

BY THE REV. ANDREW DONLEVY, LL.D.

'Hear counsel and receive instruction, that thou mayest be wise in thy latter end."—*Prov.* xix, 20.

Third Edition.

DUBLIN :

PUBLISHED FOR THE ROYAL CATHOLIC
COLLEGE OF ST. PATRICK, MAYNOOTH,

BY JAMES DUFFY, 10, WELLINGTON-QUAY.

1848.

Title page of the Dublin 1848 edition of the Donlevy Catechism

rllaṁ évṁ baıṙ ṗéın ᴅ'ḟrlaıɜ, ṙrl cıonntócaıᴅıṙ
an Aɜaıᴅ ceactaıṙ ᴅıoḃ.

C. An ḃṗrl ṙé aıṙ aṙ laıṁ-ne na Srḃaıl-
ceaᴅa aɜ ṙ na Ɗeaɜoıḃṙeaca-ṙo rle ᴅo lean-
ṁrn, aɜṙ na Peacaıᴅe ɜ ̧aıneaṁla, aıṙ aṙ
laḃṙamaṙ ᴅo ṙeacnaᴅ?

F. A tá ɜan Aṁaṙr, maılle ṙé Ɜ ̧aṙaıḃ
Ɗé.

AN 19. LÉJⅫONN.

Ɗo ɜ ̧aṙaıḃ. Ɗé.

C. Cṙeᴅ ıṙ Cıall ᴅo ɜ ̧aṙaıḃ Ɗé?

F. Cıallrɜıᴅ a ɜCoıtcınne ɜac rle caḃaṙtṙ
ᴅa ḃṙaɜamrᴅ an Aıṙɜe ó Ɗhıa; aɜṙ ɜac rle
ṁaıt ᴅa nƊeaṙnaıᴅ ɜo Ḟıalṁaṙ ᴅrnn, aɜṙ nác
aṙ trlleamaṙ aıṙ Aon-coṙ raᴅ.

C. Cá ṁéıᴅ Cıneʋl Ɜ ̧aṙ ann?

F. Jṙ ıomᴅa ṙın; a tá Crᴅ ᴅıoḃ Naᴅrṙéa,
maṙ a taıᴅ Soɜal, Slaınte, Neaṙt, Trɜṙe, &c.,
Crᴅ oıle óṙ Cıonn Naᴅrṙe, maṙ a taıᴅ Joncol-
nrɜaᴅ Ɯhıc Ɗé, Ḟ ̧aṙɜlaᴅ an Chınıᴅ Ɗonna,
&c.; a tá Crᴅ ᴅıoḃ a Ꞇoḃ a mrɜ ᴅınn, maṙ a
taıᴅ Ꞇeaɜaṙɜ an tSoıṙɜéıl, aṙ nɜaıṙrṁ évṁ an
Chṙeıᴅırṁ, &c., aɜṙ Crᴅ oıle ımṁeaᴅónac nó
Ꞇoḃ a ṙtıɜ ᴅınn, maṙ a taıᴅ Cṙeıᴅeaṁ, Ɗóccaṙ,
Ɜ ̧aᴅ, &c.

C. Cṙeᴅ ɜo ṙnṙaᴅac évɜeaṙ tr ṙé Ɜ ̧a-
ṙaıḃ Ɗé?

F. Trɜım na Tıoᴅlaıceaᴅa neaṙṙᴅa, ᴅo ᴅóıṙ-
teaṙ Ɗıa, ṙṙe na Ɯhóṙ tṙócaıṙe ṗéın, aɜṙ
maṙ ɜeall aıṙ Lraıɜeact JOSA CRJOSƊ,
ann aṙ ɜCṙoıᴅe, évṁ aṙ nɜlanta ó Pheacaᴅ,
aɜṙ évṁ ɜo ṙoıtṙeacamoıṙ an ḃeata ṁaṙ-
évnnac.

Page from the Dublin 1848 edition of the Donlevy Catechism

Imitation, and the College, Renehan says, 'encouraged both these publications engaging two hundred copies of the one, and three hundred copies of the other'. Maynooth was making good use of the books. About this time some sixty students from the Second Divinity Year attended Irish classes held in the afternoon from five to six o'clock, the text-books in use being an Irish grammar and dictionary, the New Testament and Donlevy's Irish Catechism, in the McEncroe edition no doubt.

John McEncroe was a student of the College and had begun his work on the catechism some three years before while still a student. He went to Australia and was Dean of Sydney at the time Renehan was writing his preface. The copy of McEncroe's edition I have seen is in the National Library. The title page credits Donlevy with a D.D. and acknowledges corrections from the Press by E. O'Reilly Esq., author of the Irish Dictionary, Grammar etc. The printer was Thomas Courtney of 18 Whitefriar-street and old publishing friends of the era, R. Coyne of 4 Capel-street and D. Wogan of Merchant's Quay, together with 'the principal booksellers in Ireland' are said to have it in stock. The Preface is given in English only and considerably abridged. The catechism is set page to page in Irish and English, a method adopted by Donlevy that is followed in all our bilingual catechisms. McEncroe introduced quite a number of changes in the text which Renehan was later to deplore. The catechism is followed by a Pathetic Poem, in Irish, on the Life and Sufferings of Jesus Christ and by a Compendium of Irish Grammar. The poem, it takes up some six pages of the work's 424, is prefaced with a note apologising to the subscribers for its insertion in place of their names. The editor, McEncroe explains, had been strongly advised to publish it as it was supposed to have been written by Doncha Mór O Dálaigh, Abbot of Boyle, in the 14th century. It may have appeared a poor substitute, catechetically, for O'Hussey's *Suim Bhunudhasach*, Renehan certainly thought so, but it was a link with the tradition of the later Middle Ages that was to persist in the devotion of Irish Catholics down to recent times, this preoccupation with the wounds of Christ.

The Third Edition was a return to pure Donlevy. Renehan declared his aim at 'reproducing in a convenient form,and at a very low price, Dr Donlevy's Catechism exactly as he wished it to appear'. He did just this. The author's preface is much abridged and given in English only but otherwise everything is there as Donlevy had it, including O'Hussey's verses and the elements of the Irish Language. One misses the large print of the original, the exciting script from the Paris fount and the quaint use of capitals that held one so much in the 18th century. In respect of the Irish section, however, Renehan's edition does afford a specimen, as he claims, of what the language was like a hundred years before. Perhaps this is really why he undertook the work, with a view to helping antiquarians and students of the language.[7] He acknowledges this objective in his preface, while advancing 'the vastly more important good of relieving the dearth of Irish religious books' as his chief purpose. He frankly allows that the language in his time was falling more and more into disuse. The only question was the rapidity of its decay. More than three millions of his countrymen, he felt, could still speak or understand Irish — 'the tongue which finds easiest access to their hearts'. The National Schools at this time were closing in on Irish culture and English was well established as the language of instruction. Renehan must have had his doubts.

In fact, Donlevy's catechism as a medium of religious instruction in Irish was already being supplanted, as Renehan did his work, by the 'Short Donlevy' which I call the Tuam Catechism, mentioned in the preface as having been published by Archbishop McHale in Dublin in 1843. The Tuam Catechism is the one that was to bring Donlevy as a catechetical force into this century. It came besides with Donlevy's typographical tradition. The Irish portion of the Tuam text appeared in Gaelic characters, the only shorter Irish catechism so printed from the list quoted by Renehan.[8] This link with the mother text is of special interest. It bridges the two ages of our Tridentine catechesis, the penal age and the age of freedom. Renehan notes that Donlevy's work was the last book of Catholic religious instruction printed on the continent in Irish letters and the first so printed at home (in the McEncroe edition) after the persecution.

The Third Edition was published for the Royal Catholic College of St Patrick, Maynooth, by James Duffy of 10 Wellington-Quay in Dublin, 1848. Copies are not very difficult to come by.

---

7 At the end of the century, when the revival movement was gathering its momentum, *Donlevy* continued to attract scholars as a source book for Learning the Irish Language. The Rev. William Hayden, SJ, published *An Introduction to the Study of the Irish Language based upon the Preface of Donlevy's Catechism*, Dublin, M. H. Gill and Son; London, David Nutt, 1891, pp. 69. The work consisted of the text in both languages and a Glossary.

8 Among these, O'Reilly's and the McHale catechism — Renehan makes no reference to the evident connection of both these texts with Donlevy's. Like so many of our historians he talked about the catechisms without having read them.

84

9

The Tuam Catechism

The Tuam catechism was not first published in 1843, as stated by Renehan, nor is its compilation — the Gaelic version at least — properly attributed to Archbishop MacHale, as Henry Bradshaw, the Cambridge librarian, seemed to think. The catechism first appeared in 1839, the Irish version in an attractive Gaelic script:

An Teagasg Críosdaighe: De réir chomhairle Ard-Easboig Thuama, agus Easbog na Cúige sin. A m-baile Atha-cliath; Clobhuailte le T. Coldamhell, 78 pp., 12 mo.

'Directions for Reading the Irish Language' are supplied in English.

The work came with weighty approbation: 'This is the catechism which we approve and recommend to the faithful committed to our care'. The signatures follow, of John Archbishop of Tuam, and his suffragan bishops, Thomas of Clonfert, Patrick of Achonry, Patrick of Elphin, Edmund of Kilmacduagh & Kilfenora, George of Galway, and Thomas of Killala. The Irish version: 'Molamoid an Teagasg Críosdaighe so Chum usáide na g-Creidmheach. Sheagan, Ard-Easbog Thuama'.

The texts were published separately and jointly, whether jointly at the beginning I have not been able to discover. The oldest bilingual edition I have come by is printed by C. M. Warren of 21 Upper Ormond Quay, Dublin, in 1859, the text in the Donlevy tradition, question matching question, the Irish on the left. The catechism became widely known as 'MacHale's Catechism', but the Irish text is certainly not his work. The compiler was Father Martin Loftus.

This Father Loftus had been Irish professor at Maynooth, the professorship having been set up in 1802 when Father Paul O'Brien was appointed to the chair. On his death in 1820 Father Loftus took over and was in possession for six years. At the time of the Royal Commission in 1827 he had left and the chair was vacant.[1] Loftus was subsequently parish priest of Dunmore and seems to

1 E. Cahill, SJ, 'Eclipse of the Irish Nation in the Eighteenth Century', in the *I.E.R.*, April 1943, p. 259.

have been a confidant of MacHale's. When the Archbishop was locked in battle on the National Schools issue with Murray of Dublin, two of their priests were despatched to Rome to plead the respective causes, John Ennis, the pastor of Booterstown, from Dublin, and Martin Loftus from Tuam.[2] The Franciscan scholar, Pádraig Ó Súilleabháin, unearthed a reference, of all places, in a Spanish work, about 1843 — he could not be more precise becaue the title page was missing — to a meeting of Irish bishops in Dublin of 8 November 1842 during which there was question of a New Testament in Irish, the work to be entrusted to Loftus.[3]

These biographical snippets establish that Loftus could have compiled the 'Short Donlevy' if he had a mind to. Bibliographical titbits picked up in the libraries serve to secure his title. The copy of the 1839 first edition in the National Library has an entry in long-hand on the title page, 'By Martin Loftus, P.P. Dunmore'. The copy in the Franciscan Library Killiney of the same edition belonged to the Irish scholar, Séamas Ó Casaide. It bears a note in Ó Casaide's hand-writing that another copy he (Ó Casaide) had of the catechism was similarly attributed to Loftus. There is an interesting binding of catechisms in Maynooth Library, bought from the executors of Monsignor Masterson, Dean of Ardagh, in October 1960, which includes a copy of our text, again with a long-hand insert, 'Martin Loftus' and to clinch the issue, if need be, the *Catholic Directory* for 1840, p. 307, names Loftus as responsible for the Irish portion of 'the English and Irish catechism just published in pursuance of the unanimous resolutions of the Archbishop and Bishops of Connaught'.

The *Directory* notes that 'this compilation has been selected from the best catechisms, having for its model that already in most general use in the province'. Archbishop Kelly had stated, in his evidence before the Commissioners in 1824, that Donlevy's catechism was then in use in his diocese of Tuam. The McEncroe edition had been of course available since 1822.

Loftus had done a good job. Donlevy's text was indeed his main guide. He had O'Reilly's on call too and he made judicious use of Butler's 'General' catechism, the revision issued in the early 19th century under the aegis of 'the Four Archbishops' and then widely established throughout the country.

The prayer sequence, the 'Urnaíghe na Maidne agus an Tráth-nóna' is taken from the O'Reilly booklet with the slightest variation, thus reflecting the traditional piety of our people, as yet unchanged.

2 P. C. Barry, SJ, 'The Holy See and the Irish National Schools', in *I.E.R.*, August 1959.

3 'Varia' in *Éigse*, Vol. XIV, Part II, 1971, footnote, p. 123.

86

Loftus used the singular personal pronoun in the 'Acts', as in the Gaelic versions of O'Reilly's, and unlike the English text. The English version supplied is in turn less cumbersome than O'Reilly's, who ever was responsible for this part of the work, and not in the least archaic. The 'Long Acts' and 'The Prayer to be said before Mass', already spoken of as so familiar to Tridentine worshippers for well over a century, are part of the sequence.

The catechism proper follows the structure of the tradition, the four 'things', the 'keire nehe' of the O'Reilly phonetic, together with the medieval style odds-and-ends, all set down in a straight sequence of 32 lessons, not one of them given a title. The parts are outlined in the second chapter, two questions following on the authority of the Council of Trent as justifying the division. The opening lesson emphasises the great importance of catechism, just as Donlevy does. 'What means the catechism?' 'Is it necessary to attach great respect to the catechism?' 'With what disposition should we learn the catechism?'

The answer to this latter enquiry shows how closely Loftus proposed to follow his mentor, the variation here as in so many other examples of more interest to linguists than to catechists:

D. Is cóir éisdeacht ris go hAireach, macanta, modhamhuil amhuil is dá mbeith ar d-Tighearna arna Iosa Críosd ag caint.

T. Is cóir dhuinn éisdeacht leis go h-aireach, macanta, módamhail, cho maith agus da m-beidheadh ar d-Tighearna Iosa Críost ag caint linn.

The mood of instruction thus established, the lesson breaks on to the Sign of the Cross, its significance as the sign of a Christian, how it is reverently made and how frequently it should be practised. The text reminds one here of the introductory section of the Devereux catechism in the Ferns tradition. Donlevy gives the lesson much later in his catechesis.

The third through the ninth lessons cover the nature of faith and of the creed which is its object, the text distinguishing between the kinds of faith. The treatment generally follows Donlevy very closely, frequently word for word. So closely that one immediately spots a departure, as in the fourth lesson, on the Blessed Trinity, which elects for O'Reilly's English text, 'Is the Father God? Yes, truly etc.', and in the eighth lesson on the Church where Loftus borrows the marks of the Church, if one may so put it, from Butler's 'General'.

The commandments and Church precepts follow from lesson X to lesson XX, the second thing to be done, 'Cad é an dara nidh tá riachtanach chum ár slánuighthe?' Loftus abandons the old

87

Gaelic rhymed decalogue which came down to us in An t-Athair
Peadar's text, for the emended form which follows:[4]

1. Is me-se amhain do Dhia, d'a d-tabh'rfair grádh.
2. Ainm an Tighearna Dé, ná tabh'r gan fáth.
3. Coimhéad an t-saoire naomhtha, mar is cóir.
4. Do d'athair 's do mhathair módh 'gus onóir tabh'r.
5. Na déan marbhadh, seáchain fuath 'gus fearg.
6. Na déan druis; 's na claon le gaethibh garg.
7. Na déan goid, no éagcóir, ann aon am.
8. Na tabh'r'nn aghaidh do chomharsan fiadhnuis cham.
9. Na santuigh bean do chomharsan, le do lo.
10. 'S a cuid no 'maoin na santuigh fós go deo.

It looks much better in the Gaelic script, nothing indeed to the
original Donlevy fount, but nice. The version given in the 1839
text is slightly different.

There is a peculiar verse form of the precepts also, at least in
the text I am quoting from, a C. M. Warren printing. There is
a different version in the 1839 edition, and not in verse. Loftus
has a footnote in this Warren text 'about the quaint form of reciting
the commandments of the Church familiar to the older people',
adding that it is found in 'some of our Irish catechisms'. His own
version goes like this:

1. Domhnadh 's lá saoire, aifrionn éist go beacht.
2. Troisg an caraois iomlán réir naomh reacht.
3. Na-hith feoil ar aon aoine na aon lá
   A bh-fuil air tréanas, gan aon chead, no fath.
4. Bliaghntamhail do shagart crom go h-umhal do ghlún,
   A bh-fuil aig' ughdarás éisteacht le do rún.
5. Corp do Thighearna glac faoi cháisg 's faoi sgáth
   Do chille fhéin, gan aistrughadh áit' no trá.
6. 'Sa g-carais, aidbheint agus feadh da lá dheug
   D'eis nodhlaic na bidheadh banis cruin go h-eug.

This is quaint as doggerel can be, and one tends, perhaps unfairly,
to compare with the careful, precise language of the English
version. But either way the Tuam lacks the raciness
of the older tradition. O'Reilly's 'smutty discourses, wanton looks
and lewd kisses' are smothered in 'abominable sins of the flesh'.
Take the Tuam's list of those exempt from the fast: 'Sick persons,
hard labourers, and those who are under the years prescribed by
the Church, or who are infirm from old age'. Compare with
O'Reilly's: 'Sick people, women with child, nurses, labourers, and
old persons of languishing constitutions'. And with Donlevy's most

4 The old verse supplied in a footnote.

effective: 'Sick People, weakly old Persons, young People not past one and twenty Years, Women big with Child (Mná tromthorracha), and People that labour hard'. Loftus may well have been translating from the English, the opposite experience of both O'Reilly and Donlevy. At any rate, the Tuam does sound a trifle prudish, as if Victorian mists were already beginning to descend.

Throughout the exposition of the decalogue the Tuam maintains a verbal parity with Donlevy, but ready again to benefit from Butler's catechism. Several of the formulas are borrowed from 'the General'; 'What special reward has God promised dutiful children?' 'What is the instruction of St Paul to Masters?' 'What obligation do these commandments impose on us?' The seventh and the tenth; and the answer rings familiarly in old Butlerian ears: 'To pay our lawful debts and give every man his own'.

The catechism does advert to the problem of usury which so preoccupied Donlevy. Reflecting the lingering echoes of what once had been so live an issue, the discussion is reduced to one effective formula and keeps on the safe side. The question: 'Are all frauds in buying and selling, and all other contracts, prohibited by these commandments?' And pat comes the answer: 'Yes; and especially frauds and iniquitous extortions of usurers and money lenders who carry on an unholy traffic on the miseries of the poor, Ezechiel xviii etc.'

Usurers in the Irish, so Loftus explains, are 'lucht gaimbín'; *lucht*, a class, *gaimbín*, of usury: the word *gambín* from the Latin, *cambium*, exchange or loan. The classical allusion unhappily clothing with some respectability the gombeen man's trade.

Donlevy's less colourful Irish gives *usuire* for a usurer and *usuireacht* for his profession. His concept of 'the unholy traffic' is much more wide-reaching. He defines usury as 'a Loan of Money, Corn, Butter, Meal, and such like, given principally in View of requiring or receiving some Hire, or worldly Profit in Virtue thereof' ('go mórmhór air shúil, Luach, nó Tairbhe shaoghalta air bith d'iarraidh nó d'fhághail air a shon').

A formidable list of scriptural and traditional sources, including papal decrees to 1679, are advanced in support of this teaching. It is lawful, Donlevy allows, to receive or even demand whatever profit may be due by way of interest on the loan as reparation for loss sustained by making it. But even here, one should have to point out the loss anticipated in making the loan, a loss that could not be avoided, and if it came to any hesitation about one's rights one should have to look to a wise person for a decision and stand by it. Hire purchase is entirely out, 'for it is Usury to sell any Thing dearer than it is actually worth, upon the sole Account of giving Credit or Time for Payment of the Price thereof'; not a bad definition of what we call hire purchase.

Donlevy taught and proposed as Church teaching that loans should be made principally out of charity, friendship or kindness, a view that must have appeared naive to many, even at a time before the virtually *laissez-faire* view of interest-taking had become so widely accepted.[5]

Reverting to the structure of our Tuam catechism, we find the 'Counsels' of Christ called 'Evangelical' considered by way of conclusion to this section on law. The two lessons following, XXI and XXII, present the theology of sin, the definition reflecting the 'General's' lordly rhythms, 'a voluntary transgression of the commandments', in place of the earlier texts' simple 'disobedience'. The seven 'Capital Sins' are given the strong presence they receive throughout the tradition, each 'source' or 'root' of evil carefully defined. Unlike O'Reilly, Donlevy examines the opposite virtues in each case, the Tuam bringing the opposing virtues together in one formula at the end, 'What are the virtues that are opposed to the seven capital sins?' It would seem that where space was scarce the accommodation was given to vice.

Further categories of sin follow, the sins against the Holy Spirit and the four sins 'that cry to heaven for vengeance'. All three texts consider the nine ways whereby one may participate in the sin of another, formidable moral risks of sinning indirectly by counsel, command, consent, provocation, praise or flattery, concealment, silence, partaking, defence of the evil done. The Tuam rounds them up: 'May not one be partaker, or become guilty of the sins of another?'

Lesson XXIII embraces the list of virtues and good works, the Tuam leading off with a formula of its own: 'Since we are bound to avoid sin and to fulfil the commandments, does not that show that we are obliged to practise good works?' Of course it does; 'certainly', 'taisbánann go cinnte'. There is instruction on praying for the dead and offering Mass for the souls in purgatory. The

5 It was never Church teaching that interest is in itself wrong, as Donlevy implies, but moralists and confessors were sharply divided about the conditions that would make it justifiable. In the 19th century, Roman Congregations, in the course of a number of decisions, stated that those who lend money at a moderate rate of interest were 'not to be disturbed'. The decisions were tentative, however, in the sense that the faithful were expected to be willing to abide by any future decisions the Holy See might make. The usury controversy continues and has become an issue of increasing urgency. For a series of articles by Conway, Rev P. on 'some recent Catholic Opinions on Interest-Taking', see *I.E.R.*, Sept. 1942 to Febr. 1943.

virtues are recited, 'theological' and 'cardinal', and the lesson rounded off with the Beatitudes, the high point of the Sermon on the Mount.

Lessons XXIV through XXIX cover the third thing necessary for salvation, the reception of the sacraments. Loftus has his own rhyme in Irish for numbering the sacraments. What one notices particularly here is the Tuam's participation in the advance of 'theologising' that was to do such damage to catechesis in the 19th century. There is a formula, indeed it must be allowed, closely following the *Roman Catechism* 'How many things are necessary for a sacrament? Three things, viz. matter, form and the intention of the Church'. And as a further example of the later seminary textbook theology in our elementary instruction, distinction is made between sacraments of the living and sacraments of the dead, sacraments that may be received once only and so on.

In the lesson on Confirmation, the last question, 'Is it a sin to neglect confirmation, when there is an opportunity of receiving it?' is based on Butler's 'General'. The Tuam's answer: 'Yes; especially in those evil days of persecution and seduction', does seem for its time to over-emphasise the concept of Confirmation as a 'persecution' sacrament.

The treatment of the Blessed Eucharist in the lesson that follows is structured like the 'General', first as a sacrament, where Donlevy is followed almost verbatim, and then as a sacrifice where the 'General' is the guide. Loftus provides his own definition of a sacrifice and his own words in explaining how the Mass is the same sacrifice as that of the cross.

The 'Fourth Thing' necessary, to put our hope in God and to crave his assistance in prayer, is the business of the three remaining lessons. The petitions of the *Our Father* are detailed as in Donlevy's. The *Hail Mary* instruction is so modelled also, and the Rosary, recommended as the most usual devotion in honour of Our Lady. This from the 1839 Gaelic version:

C. Cia an urnaighe is gnáthach lin a rádh a n-onóir na Maighdine Muire?
F. An Paidrín, sé sin, an Choróin Muire.

The 'Directions for Reading the Irish Language' are given at the end of the booklet in all the Tuam texts, Donlevy having done the same with his 'Elements of the Irish Language', and likewise William Williams in his edition of O'Reilly's catechism. '*Irish-Men* without *Irish*', Donlevy archly remarked, 'is an Incongruity, and a great Bull'. But it was an incongruity suffered peacefully in those days by an increasing number of the Irish, especially the educated ones. Donlevy's 'Community Boys' were not the only

91

clergy in Ireland with the pastoral disadvantage of knowing nothing but a foreign tongue.[6]

How faithful were the Archbishops and Bishops of the province of Tuam to their catechism? It certainly had a long innings. But when the new national text, *A Catechism of Catholic Doctrine*, was taking over in the 1950s the Butler 'Maynooth Catechism' had been in possession throughout Connaught, for how long and how precisely from diocese to diocese I cannot say. The Loftus catechism, however, had not been entirely replaced; it was still in use in the Connemara Gaeltacht. It was a tenuous survival and, it apart, all that was left of the Donlevy tradition in the province in those latter years was the format of the O'Flaherty bilingual edition of the Butler usurper, sponsored by the diocese of Elphin, the Irish in Gaelic script on the left side, the English on the right, question opposite question.

Library copies of the Tuam catechisms are plentiful. I have found copies in the National Library, the Franciscan Library in Killiney, the Cork and Galway University Libraries, Maynooth, Thurles College; my own copy of the first Irish printing, in microfilm, from the Bradshaw Collection in Cambridge. But outside the libraries copies are not easily come by, one never finds one, at least I never have, in the antiquarian catalogues, booklets of the sort were so flimsy and expendable.

6 Respecting the fate of the Irish language, see E. Cahill, SJ, quoted above, also *I.E.R.*, articles by the same author, June 1940, 'The Irish Language in the Penal Era', July, 1940, 'Irish Scholarship in the Penal Era', September 1943 and February 1944, 'Ireland in the Nineteenth Century'.

In the Penal Era article, Cahill refers to Donlevy's statement in his Preface to the catechism that he wrote the English text 'in favour of those who speak only English'. He thinks this suggests that Donlevy who was away from Ireland for 31 years mistakenly thought that a considerable number of Catholics at the time did not speak Irish and that of those who did a certain percentage were unable to read it, although they were able to read English. The truth, however, would seem to emerge from Cahill's own study that many of those educated in the popular schools had not been taught to read or write Irish.

Epilogue

A profusion of texts was a problem from earliest days. Some thirty-nine Protestant catechisms have been listed as published before Luther produced his Large and Little catechisms in 1529. [1] The Catholic position was the same. The catechisms of Canisius and Bellarmine that we have called our prototypal texts had as one of their aims the displacement of others. The Emperor Ferdinand wanted one catechism for all his subjects and apparently envisaged the *Summa Doctrinae Christianae* as suitable for children of all grades.[2] Canisius had more realistic plans; but the emphasis was on unity. Pope Clement VIII was the patron of Bellarmine's catechisms and backed them with a papal brief. The Pope spoke of his concern about the number of different catechisms in use which was 'giving rise to no little difficulty and confusion in both teaching and learning'. The brief prescribed Bellarmine's work for sole use in Rome and its environs and strongly recommended its adoption 'in every part of the world'. In 1663 Pope Urban VIII recommended it for the mission fields, and in 1742 Benedict XIV addressed a special constitution to all the bishops of the Church reiterating the advice of Clement VIII that Bellarmine's should be the official manual of every diocese. And Pius IX, at the first Vatican Council, pushed for the issue of a universal catechism, with Bellarmine's as the basis of the work.[3]

These papal aspirations were not to be fulfilled but their continuing presence promoted the idea of containing the spread of catechisms. The 'Maynooth Catechism' in the Butler tradition, fruit of the 1875 plenary synod of the Irish bishops, was our first joint effort to provide a national catechism acceptable to all. The Wallace thesis uncovers interesting evidence about the physical

1 E. Magenot, *Dictionnaire de Théologie Catholique*, coll. 1902-1917, quoted in the commentary on the *Catechesi Tradendae* of Pope John Paul 11, St Paul Editions, Boston, U.S.A., 1980.

2 Ferdinand's edict, 14 August 1554, introducing the *Summa*. F. Streicher, SJ, *S. Petri Canisii Catechismi Latini et Germanici, Societatis Jesu Selecti Scriptores*, Vol. 11, t.ii, Pars Prima, Catechismi Latini, Rome, 1933.

3 James Brodrick, SJ, *The Life and Work of Blessed Robert Francis Cardinal Bellarmine, SJ*, London, 1928, Vol. 1, pp. 395f.

origins of this revision of Butler's 'General', the source being the archives of the Dublin publishers, M. H. Gill and Son.[4] A deal was struck for the publishing rights of the catechism in 1882 between the firm and Bishop Patrick Moran (later the Australian Cardinal), acting on behalf of the hierarchy. So the 'Maynooth' was launched seven years after the synod; but by 1889 Mr Gill had reason to be grumpy about his bargain. He complained in a letter to the secretary of the hierarchy in June of that year that he naturally understood, from the title of the catechism, that it would be generally used, whereas many dioceses never used it and others that commenced to use it had given it up. What exactly went wrong?

In an *Irish Ecclesiastical Record* article of January 1892, 'Our Catechisms: Is there room for improvement?', very critical of the 'Maynooth', Archbishop Walsh of Dublin, who had been an official at the synod, questioned the authenticity of the titlepage which claimed that the catechism had been 'ordered by the National Synod of Maynooth, and approved by the Cardinal, the Archbishops, and the Bishops of Ireland for general use throughout the Irish Church'. In Walsh's view the catechism 'in no way emanated from the Maynooth synod', meaning, as he explained, that it was never considered for approval by the Fathers of the synod nor even examined, and that there is no reference to it in the synodal decrees. It was a lawyer's judgment.

Walsh's interpretation of the minutes of the meetings is that when the question of the catechism came up the Fathers referred it to a sub-committee without any decision. In due course the sub-committee produced a copy of the text for the synod's secretary, whereupon the Fathers decided that a copy should be made available to each bishop. This was not done for lack of time and, in Walsh's view, there the matter rested. I think he was right.[5]

---

4 Op. cit., ms. pp. 111f., 144f, 161f.

5 See *Acta et Decreta Synodi Plenariae Episcoporum Hiberniae Habitae apud Maynutiam, An. MDCCCLXXV*. Dublini: Typis Browne et Nolan. MDCCCLXXVII. The secretary of the synod was the bishop of Ardagh, Dr Conroy, assisted by two officials, Drs Walsh and Molloy. Bishop Moran was president of the subcommittee dealing with matters of Faith, and so with the catechism. Dr Walsh's argument was that 'whatever may have been the nature of the approval subsequently given to this edition of the Catechism, the edition itself in no way emanated from the Maynooth Synod': pp. 52-54, *Acta et Decreta*, the first item recorded in the minutes of the *Congregatio Privata Decimasexta*, the last of these sessions:

> Parvus Catechismus a Deputatione de fide redactus, coram Patribus delatus est a Secretario: quem proelo subjiciendum statuerunt Patres ut singulis

The evidence is confusing but the truth would seem to be that the catechism's claim to have been prescribed for the whole country was due more to Bishop Moran's zeal and determination and his personal involvement in the project than to the commitment of the bishops in general to a national catechism binding on all. Hesitation at the synod and the ambiguity of procedure were rooted in a principle of the Tridentine institution which the Irish Church quickly grasped and jealously guarded. It is the principle of a bishop's right, without prejudice to general law, of judging in given circumstances what is best for his flock. Cardinal Consalvi used the principle adroitly in the affair of the catechism of Napoleon. The French bishops would not be forced to elect for the uniform catechism; their liberty of choice would not be taken from them.[6] Archbishop Troy, on the other hand, in his peculiar difficulty after the 1798 rebellion, would no doubt have wished that he might have been able to prescribe the Butler 'General' throughout the kingdom; he had been the most closely associated with the venture and had seen to it that the revised catechism had the appropriate political orientations as he adjudged them. But he too acknowledged the principle and he had, of course, enough evidence to make him aware that if he had attempted otherwise a considerable number of his colleagues would not have been with him.

Hence, when the 'Maynooth' was ultimately published under synodal 'order', there were many bishops unwilling to adopt it. Gill and Son did better by their contract as the years went on, the uniforming urge rather than neglect of the principle adding further subscribers; but they did nothing as well as they had hoped, and had indeed been led to believe: in 1951, when the firm were in trade again with *A Catechism of Catholic Doctrine*, 'Approved by the Archbishops and Bishops of Ireland', 15 of the 27 dioceses had not been using the Maynooth Catechism.

The 1951 text was meant to be a national catechism — on this

Episcopis examplaria mitterentur, quod tamen ob defectum temporis fieri non potuit.

One gets the impression of some haste and flurry to get the business finished. Arrangements were to be made for the submission of the synodal decrees to the Holy See and for the correction and publication of the Pastoral Letter prepared for issue to the faithful after the synod. Something had to be done about a 'novum quoddam genus minus honeste saltandi, jam in Hibernia invalescens'. The problem of priests 'qui vitio ebrietatis infeliciter addicti' and where to house them. Should a C.C. have to ask his P.P's permission to be out of the house for the night? Sufficient to notify the pastor; this decision incorporated in Statute 223. But not a word about the *Parvus Catechismus* in either statutes or index.

6 Wallace ms. cit., p. 145.

occasion there was no controversy — yet it was not published as prescribed. So far, indeed, from being insensitive to the principle, the co-ordinators of the revision enshrined it in one of their formulas:

161. What is the authority of the bishop in his own diocese? The bishop in his own diocese has power from God to teach, to sanctify and to rule the faithful, in subjection to the Pope,and in accordance with the laws of the Church.

And, in the event, the uniforming zeal that brought the new catechism into being collapsed before this principle of a bishop's rights in his own diocese when difficulties arose about the way the catechism ought to be presented. Our Tridentine era came to an end with as many editions of the new catechism as we had catechisms themselves before the uniform text was finally agreed upon.

Dissatisfaction not only with the format of the new catechism but with its wording and even its content arose from another problem that surfaced from earliest times and was more fundamental than the multiplicity of texts; it turned on the limitations of the genre itself. How fruitful was the catechetical method proving to be with children and simple folk?

Canisius was certainly unhappy with a system of instruction confined almost completely to technical theological formulas. Otherwise he would not have promoted the catechism-cum-prayerbook idea, nor would he have bothered to illustrate his texts so profusely. No doubt he accepted the subject-centred, deductive educational approach, but he was concerned with childrens' difficulties. His English-language biographer, James Brodrick, tells how he never wearied, amid all his other duties, of revising and improving his little catechisms, and there's a lovely story of Canisius, at seventy-five, in the last year of his life, preparing an edition of the 'Shortest Catechism' with the words divided into syllables, 'to enable my dear little children to learn it more easily'.[7]

It was a kindly thought, and God knows they needed it. 'The Shortest' consisted of 59 questions and answers, the answers often running to forty words or more. Here is an example:

11. Is it sufficient for a Christian to believe what the creed comprises?

No indeed, because the Christian faith embraces not only those truths expressed by the creed but such in general as are contained in all the books of divine scripture; those, moreover, that are properly deduced,

7 James Brodrick, SJ, *Saint Peter Canisius SJ*, London, 1939, p. 239.

as it were from founts, partly from the articles of the creed and partly from the sacred scriptures; and, finally, such as the Holy Spirit bears witness to and teaches through the Church as belonging to the faith. 'If he will not hear the Church, let him be to thee as the heathen and the publican', says the gospel.

This was straight-forward enough compared to definitions such as:

31. What is a sacrament?

It is an external and visible sign of divine and invisible grace, divinely instituted, so that in it one receives the grace of God and sanctification. Thus, as the infant is washed with water in the sacred font, so is this an effective sign that the infant's soul within is cleansed, that is purified and made holy.

The multiplication of formulas of this kind, which reached its peak in our experience in the 'Maynooth', so incensed Archbishop Walsh that he described the burden placed on children as 'little short of cruelty'.[8]

The Archbishop was writing in the climate of a continuing, if intermittent, movement of protest against an unduly technical style of instruction. The movement kept running through Tridentine times, but I mention by way of example the *Historical Catechism*

---

8   The translation, as it might have been done, had we adopted the catechism, from Streicher's critical text of the *minimus* in the original Latin, *Summa Doctrinae Christianae, per quaestiones tradita et ad captum rudiorum accommodata*:

> 11. Estne satis christiano ea credere, quae complectitur symbolum?
>
> Non sane, quia fides christiana non tantum circa isthaec, quae symbolo expressa sunt, sed etiam in universum circa illa versatur, quae divinae scripturae libris omnibus continentur; deinde quae partim ex symboli articulis, partim ex scripturis sacris veluti fontibus rite deducuntur; postremo, quae ad fidem spectare testatur ac docet per ecclesiam Spiritus sanctus. 'Si quis autem ecclesiam non audierit, sit tibi sicut ethnicus et publicanus', inquit evangelium.
>
> 31. Quid est sacramentum?
>
> Est divinae et invisibilis gratiae externum et visibile signum divinitus institutum, ut in eo quis Dei gratiam accipiat atque sanctificationem. Ut, cum in sacro fonte abluitur infans aqua, signum hoc est efficax infantis animam intus ablui, id est purificari atque sanctificari.

Although the *minimus* had only 59 formulas to the 'Short Maynooth's' 156, each had the same number of words, c. 2,500. The *minor*, on the other hand, the *Capita Doctrinae Christianae, compendio tradita, ut sit veluti Parvus Catechismus Catholicorum*, corresponding to the full text of the 'Maynooth', with 124 formulas to the latter's 426, was much the shorter of the two, some 5,500 words as against 12,500. The short catechisms of the Butler tradition, moreover, consisted of a selection of formulas extracted from the full text, whereas the wording of the *minimus* and the *minor* varied considerably.

97

of the French catechist, Claude Fleury, which first appeared in 1683 with the approbation of the Bishop of Meaux who is known to history as Bossuet. The English version of Fleury's catechism 'containing a Summary of the Sacred History and Christian Doctrine' had an impressive printing history in Dublin. The first printing I can trace was for Bartholomew Gorman, Bookseller, at the Bible, in Bridge-Street, near Cook-Street, in 1763. I hold a copy of this edition. The Franciscan Library in Killiney has a 1776 printing by Pat Wogan, and one can trace a flurry of repeats throughout the first half of the century following, e.g., Wogan, 1811; Coyne, 1828; Catholic Book Society, 1837; Grace, 1843.

Fleury's elaborate 'Discourse concerning the Design and Use of this catechism' expounds the theory of protest. His objection to the accustomed style of catechisms goes like this:

The words *essence* and *subsistence*, signify quite another thing to the people, than to the learned. Act, power, quality, disposition, habitual, virtual; all these words which signify abstractions or second intentions, as they are called in the schools, are a language not to be understood by the generality of Christians. We might as well let them say the creed in Latin, as expound it to them in this sort. Experience makes it evident. When you have wearied yourself with making children or peasants to repeat a hundred times; that in God there are three persons in one nature, and in Jesus Christ two natures in one person; as often as you shall ask the question you will put them to the hazard of saying, two persons in one nature, or three natures in one person.

The *Historical Catechism*, in two versions, the short and the long, is made up of biblical narratives and doctrinal lessons. Each lesson of the short version is followed by a little catechism of questions and answers bearing on the text; 'I have made the answers', Fleury says, 'as short as I could, the less to weary the children, and the more to imitate nature: for they speak not much at a time'.

As the second half of the century approached, the position of the Butler catechisms was being consolidated with heavy printings of the 'General' and from 1882 the 'Maynooth' making the progress it did.[9] The principle of including the question in the

9 The printing history of the 'General' is not without some evidence of awareness on the lines we have been discussing. The National Library has an interesting 12th edition, Cork, Printed and Sold by Geary, Bookseller, Exchange, 1829. An appendix of prayers and devotions following the text, including the Christian's Daily Exercise not, as later, in question and answer form but as an exhortation in the O'Reilly tradition. A Daily Meditation at the back of the title page is a nice summary of Tridentine piety:

O Christians, remember that you have today
A God to glorify, a Jesus to imitate,

answer, making the answer a statement in itself, was adopted by the 'Maynooth', and this was a good thing; but it did make the answers longer and, with no accommodation in respect of so many difficult words, the effect was cumbersome.

Dr Walsh felt that a collection of 426 such formulas was too much of a good thing and he wanted it replaced in Dublin by a catechism to his own liking. The diocesan committee that had been working on the project for some time had a draft catechism ready by 1896 with a series of 'Lessons on the Catechism' which consisted of an exposition of the main themes and was meant to precede the learning of the formulas. This was a fall-back on Fleury's principle, though Walsh's simplified 'Butler' (the choice of language similar to that of the bishops' 'national' that was to follow 55 years later) and the reduced number of formulas — about a 100 less than in the 'Maynooth' — made no provision for the scripture narratives in the catechism structure itself. The Catholic Truth Society of Ireland issued the lessons in a booklet in 1904 but the catechism was never published.[10]

Archbishop Walsh's failed protest was not, however, the end of the matter. In 1934 Michael Sheehan, a former Maynooth professor, then coadjutor Archbishop of Sydney, produced in

> The intercession of the angels and saints
> to invoke,
> A soul to save, a body to mortify,
> Sins to expiate, virtues to acquire,
> A hell to avoid, a heaven to gain,
> An eternity to prepare for, a short time
> to husband well,
> A neighbour to edify, a world to despise,
> Devils to combat, passions to subdue,
> And perhaps death to suffer and judgment
> to undergo.

10   For the history of the catechism project see the *I.E.R.* for comment on the Archbishop's article, 1892 and again in 1896 when the draft was on offer. *The Lessons on the Catechism*, the work of Monsignor Gerald Molloy, presumably that Dr Molloy who shared the assistant secretaryship at the synod with Dr Walsh, covers the material of the catechism and follows its order, but has 54 lessons to the catechism's 42 chapters. See also Patrick J. Walsh, *William J. Walsh, Archbishop of Dublin*, Dublin & Cork, 1928, pp. 379-386. Besides the *Catechism of Christian Doctrine for Primary Schools*, all set and ready for issue by Browne and Nolan, there was an *Elementary Catechism of Christian Doctrine*, which I have not seen but take to be the 'Short' edition. Walsh says that publication was suspended when the idea of a national text was again mooted at the approach of the 1900 plenary synod, and when that was held and nothing happened the scheme was abandoned on hearing that Pius X had a universal catechism in mind. Perhaps the real reason is that the archdiocese had proved unwilling to accept change.

Ireland *A Child's Book of Religion*, 'For use in the Home and School', the publishers Gill of Dublin. Gill had already published, at the end of the first war, Sheehan's two years' course of religious instruction for our secondary schools and colleges, *Apologetics and Catholic Doctrine*, which was the kernel of the national programme. The 'Child's Book', in two parts also, was a catechism of dialogue between teacher and child reminiscent of Bellarmine's *Explicatio*, though much less technical, the dialogue interspersed with prayers and devotions. In 1938 Sheehan published, again by Gill, *A Simple Course of Religion* for primary school children. It consisted of 30 expository lessons, each followed by a prayer and a series of testing questions based on the matter outlined, Fleury's method again, except that his questions were given brief set answers. An Irish version of the 'Simple Course' was published by the Stationery Office in Dublin in 1950, *Cúrsa Simplidhe sa Chreideamh*, the translator, Micheál Ó Cionnfhaolaidh. These books had a considerable sale and must have made an impact. It was during the years of their circulation that the idea of a national catechism to replace the existing texts was revived. Unfortunately, Sheehan's work was not to influence the new catechism project in the slightest degree.

Thrusting forward to the national catechism's brief span and the revolutionary changes in the teaching of the faith that came with Vatican II, a word might be said about developments in the wider educational sphere that led, in terms of our Irish experience, to 'the new curriculum' in the national schools. The transition from the subject-centred to the child-centred elementary teaching happened so quickly that one is tempted to overlook the preparatory protest period that reaches back to the 'age of enlightenment'. The essential protest was against 'catechizing', which was used as the method of instruction not only for religion but for a wide range of subjects — history, geography, nature study, whatever. With the progress and organisation of popular education and the establishment of the inspectorate, the teachers' care that they should not be drawn beyond the limits of their knowledge amounted to an understanding that children should not be expected to know an iota more than they were formally taught. The Swiss innovator, Pestalozzi, put it brilliantly. Teachers, he said, 'would rather see one fish in their pond, than a lake full of carp the other side of the mountains'.[11] At least they were sure of their fish; they dare

11 Johann Heinrich Pestalozzi, *How Gertrude Teaches her Children*, from the German, by Holland and Turner, London, 1894, p. 51. Pestalozzi (1746-1827) published the work in 1801.

not risk the official inquisitor 'going outside the course', testing a child's native intelligence and power of observation, appealing to the imagination and feeling. It became an axiom that children could only be expected to know what they had been taught to repeat by heart.

But Pestalozzi did allow a certain merit to catechizing in that 'it is a preparatory exercise for the gradual clearing up of ideas, that it presents separate words and sentences clearly, one by one, to the sense-impression of the child'.[12] By way of example, he spoke of his teaching natural science in propositions which the children read and repeated and learned off without having the slightest idea of what they meant. And he goes on:

It was at first, like all catechisms, a mere parrot-like repetition of dull uncomprehended words. But the sharp separation of single ideas, the definite arrangement in this separation, and the consciousness deeply and indelibly impressed of these dull words, glowing in the midst of their dullness with a gleam of light and elucidation, brought them gradually to a feeling of truth and insight into the subject lying before them, that bit by bit cleared itself like sunlight from densest mist.[13]

Here, while denouncing parrotry, he was using parrot-like repetition as his point of departure and leading his 'parrots' to a grasp of truth. In 'Butler's' heyday many of our catechists were able to do this and, given the subject, I think the experience matches Pestalozzi's exactly.

The first draft of the proposed new catechism came to my attention, if I remember rightly, in the early 1940s. A committee to monitor the project had been set up by the bishops consisting of some Maynooth professors. The draft was the work of Dr William Moran, a theologian with an incisive style. It was a dialogue of some 540 questions and answers, expounding the faith in logical order and in the plainest language; the occasional lapse into an abrupt and even crude simplicity must have been enough to seal its fate:

Q. Would it be a sin to neglect to receive Confirmation?

A. It would if it could be got.

But Moran's work had possibilities. Tidied up, it was printed in 1947 by Philip Son and Nephew of Liverpool for the Catholic Mission of Calabar in British West Africa, with Bishop Moynagh's *Imprimatur*. A second edition appeared in 1953 under the

12 Op. cit., p. 45.
13 Op. cit., p. 32.

patronage of the Bishop of Meath. Both editions carried an introductory note to teachers, suggesting that when using the catechism with senior classes they would read the author's *What is Christianity?*, a series of lessons published in 1942 by the Catholic Truth Society of Ireland. The style of the lessons would envisage advanced grammar school students; but granted this, it was back to Fleury, an exposition followed by a simple catechism.

The next draft was prepared by the education professor at Maynooth, Dr Martin Brenan, who was also a lecturer in Catechetics. This draft, in more measured Tridentine style, had 444 formulas, alternative renderings frequently supplied. The comments were such as to convince the author that it would be quite futile to pursue his work further; he sent a strong letter, so he told me early in 1946, to Archbishop McQuaid of Dublin, who by this time had apparently become the patron of the new catechism proposal, suggesting that the bishops solve the matter by preparing a revision of the 'Maynooth' themselves.

The Episcopal Committee's draft was submitted to each bishop in September 1948 with the request to reply, before 1 October, to this one question: 'Is this Draft Catechism considered to be a better Catechism than that at present used in the diocese?' The replies were apparently satisfactory, for by the end of November the draft was in circulation with a request for recommendations by 1 March 1949. The catechism was published by Gill in August 1951.

A Catechism of Catholic Doctrine was an adequate, if unexciting, production, 443 formulas, all numbered and sensibly expressed.[14] It was generally accepted as an improvement, but failure to provide the 'Short' version, which dioceses using the larger Butler texts had been accustomed to for years, created a problem. This curious omission was to lead to a new kind of diversity. Bishops took to issuing their own First Communion and Short versions, 'extracted' from the official text; Fallon of Dublin printed one of these for the Raphoe diocese in Irish and English; Cork, Galway, Ossory, Tuam, Kilmore, Elphin had their versions, printed locally. This development put the idea into the heads of some diocesan inspectors, at any rate into the head of one of them, that the new catechism might benefit from a bit of editing. *My First Catechism*, 'A Book of Religion for Young Children' was published by Browne and Nolan Limited of Dublin in 1953. The text linked up with

14 For my contribution to the making of a new catechism, see *I.E.R.*, February, March, April 1949, and in the same journal my review of the catechism when published, February and March 1952.

the children's bible history, the formulas selected from the new catechism were interspersed with lesson material and the little book was richly illustrated in four colours; a new dimension in our experience, it was widely used throughout the country and had modest sales abroad, especially in South Africa. Two other booklets of this class were subsequently published, one in Cork and one in Athlone (St Paul Publications) under the auspices of the Bishop of Meath. *My First Catechism* was followed by a corresponding large version, *Catechism for Children*, also published by Browne and Nolan. This booklet, in the catechism-cum-prayer-book style of the other, was able to eliminate over 100 formulas of the official text by using lesson material in varying ways. It was illustrated in two colours by the notable Dublin priest-painter, Jack Hanlon, and was very successful.

Catechism for Children was translated into Irish by priests of the diocese of Kerry and published in 1959 by Limerick Leader Limited, *Teagasc Críostaí do Leanaí*, nicely illustrated in black and white. For the record, there were several Irish versions of the official text. A translation into northern Irish, published by Gill for the diocese of Raphoe, appeared in 1959. The Tuam version was published by Ó Gormáin Teó, Gaillimh, in 1961, and in 1964 Gill published the *Caiticiosma Teagaisc Chaitlichí* for the diocese of Dublin. All these printings had the fine large type of the English text; the Tuam and Raphoe used the Gaelic script, the Dublin the Roman. The Tuam and Raphoe texts were illustrated, the latter with the pictures from Gill's stock that were used in the English original.

The Second Vatican Council brought the new national catechism along with the era to an end. Now, with some twenty years of child-centred instruction behind us, there must be people who have their doubts about life without abstractions and who may well be yearning for those dull words of Pestalozzi's that can be made to glow with a gleam of light.

But it is a new era, a new civilisation; and the Church today has a mandate for a new presentation of the faith 'predominantly pastoral in character' and reflecting the medicine of mercy rather than of severity, as Pope John XXIII envisaged it in his opening address to the Council. There can, therefore, be no going back to the sort of catechisms we have been examining. For us the question has to turn on the survival of the genre itself: whether it is possible to find in some concept of 'the catechism' a satisfactory guide to living the faith in our time. The issue has nothing to do with 'turning back the clock'; it is a reasonable question of method. Indeed in the light of their post-Conciliar experience of catechesis, the faithful may well be crying out for catechism, crying out, even the young, for truth defined and sin identified.[15]

15 See Michael Tynan, *Catechism for Catholics: A guide to living the Faith in our time*, Dublin, Four Courts Press, 1983.

Index